HIGH ON
A LIE

A True Story

DANNY R. COX

The names and descriptions of many of the people in this book have been changed to protect their identities.

Unless otherwise noted, Scripture quotations are taken from the *New King James Version* of the Bible. Copyright© 1994, Thomas Nelson, Inc., Publishers.

10 09 08 07   10 9 8 7 6 5 4 3 2 1

High on a Lie: A True Story
978-1-949231-07-6
Copyright © 2007 by Danny R. Cox
P.O. Box 353
Troy, IL 62294

Published by Victory Graphics and Media
9731 East 54th Street
Tulsa, OK 74146
www.victorygraphicsandmedia.com

Front Cover Art: Dale Shelton

Acknowledgments

Help comes in many different shapes and forms, and no matter how much I try I will inevitably forget to mention someone who was indispensable in their part (no matter how small or large) in the writing of this book.

I would like to thank God for giving me a new life and prompting me in the spirit to put on paper what was in my heart, even though my heart was broken several times before I could finish the first chapter because the first chapter was the hardest. I would like to thank Gary Fears for his support. I want to thank Mark and Jane Dufner for making it possible to visit with my wife and children on numerous occasions along with Saundra Darrah. Thanks to my wife, Sandy, for being my best friend and an honest critic (if you are married you know how difficult that is).

I want to thank Kevin Cole for his prayers and being the biggest fan of my testimony. His encouragement has been an inspiration to me. Thanks to Bob Darrah for pushing me to get on with the book so much that I finally did. Thanks to Bill Gerard for his hours of constructive editing in my first and second writing of the book and for his continual praise of my efforts. I needed that dearly. Thanks to Bob White for teaching me how to pray and for the hours and hours of teaching me in the Word of God.

Thanks to Skip Olson, Reid Preuss, Terry Metcalf, John Spengler, John Skubish, George Lee, and John Martinez for their support to my family in my absence.

I want to say a "special thanks" to Chris Pendleton, my sister-in-law, for all the effort she put forth to help with our son, Garrett. Thanks for the pictures. We will treasure them for a lifetime. Thanks to Nancy Rydgig for her Christian support during the most trying time in my life.

Thanks to my mother for always being there and never making me feel like a loser even when I was.

Special thanks to Anna Grabowski for visiting me all over the country as well as the many letters of encouragement. Thanks for the typing book. God bless you for donating a microwave for my cell in the county jail when the one there broke.

Thanks to those who have driven countless miles and paid large phone bills and sent financial blessings to me in their kindness.

Thanks to everyone who has had so much as a kind thought, word, or deed toward me and my family. May God return your kindness one-hundredfold.

Foreword

The story that is written is true. I have known Danny personally during the years of his disobedience and now since he has come to a transformation in Christ.

It's an amazing thing to see, 'first hand', a miracle! It is even more amazing when you know, 'first hand', the individual and the circumstances. What you are about to read is a true story of miracles in every dimension. Physical impossibilities, spiritual darkness and bondage so deep as to be hopeless, time tables changed, and a life transformed. It is truly an amazing grace.

It is common today to believe we can 'reason' our way through most everything. In other words, there is not great need for faith. Yet by faith we discover a whole new world. It is God's world where the unexplainable happens frequently; where the unexpected people become the recipients of God's anointing and abundant grace.

I have read the U.S. District Court documents in which Danny's physical condition is addressed. Three separate doctors reached the same conclusion in their diagnosis. It was ALS (Lou Gehrig's disease) and it was terminal. The fact that he is alive today can only be understood as a miracle from God.

The pages before you will inspire your faith to believe God can do anything through you if you will give your life to Him.

C. Dale Edwards
Sr. Pastor
O'Fallon Assembly of God Church

Dedication

Without question I dedicate this book to my beautiful wife Sandy.

———————

Only God knows how much she has sacrificed to be
my wife and the mother of our children. She is everything
I could ever want or need in a wife and a best friend.

Contents

CHAPTER 1

I Still Miss Him

Even as a young boy of about five or six, I remember lying in bed and hearing the sound of my drunken father's fist smashing against my mother's face. Fear gripped my heart. Many mornings I would go into the kitchen for breakfast and see my mother's black eyes and swollen face. I saw the pain in her eyes as tears streamed down her cheeks while she hugged me.

My older brother, two younger sisters, and I were all terrified when our dad was drunk. He was a mean alcoholic. We were so scared when he was screaming and beating our mother that we cried out in our beds. When we did this he would yell out, "If you kids don't shut up, you will be next." We would bury our faces in our pillows to stifle the sound of our crying.

To my knowledge the only people whom my father ever hurt when he was drunk were the ones who loved him the most: his wife and children. My dad was an over-the-road truck driver. He would be on the road for weeks at a time before he came home. But when he came home he wanted to unwind and relax and have a beer. With every beer he got meaner and meaner.

I remember how much I wanted to help my mother. I thought, *when I get big enough, I'm going to beat him up good. I'm going to get even with him for all the mean things he does to my mom.*

The apostle Paul talks about this situation in Ephesians. "And you, fathers, do not provoke your children to wrath, but bring them up in the training and admonition of the Lord" (Ephesians 6:4). My father provoked his children and did not train us up in the Lord. Even at five or six, I had been provoked and was ready to return evil for evil.

And the saddest part is that even though I was afraid of my dad, I still loved him with every fiber in my being. I needed to love him and I needed him to love me, but he never showed me the love and affection that I so deeply craved. Instead, I made a vow that when I got big like him I would teach him a lesson for what he had done to my mother.

By the time I was nine years old, my mother couldn't live in fear and pain any longer. One day we came home from school and she was packed and ready to leave my dad. We went to California to live with my mother's brother and there we were safe from my dad.

However, my plans to get even with my dad when I got older wouldn't come to pass. On July 8, 1959, my dad was killed in a one-car accident. I was eleven years old.

My dad was driving home from work and he hit a concrete embankment under a state highway. The impact crushed his chest and broke his neck. Years later I asked my mother if he was drunk when he had the wreck. She said she didn't know. In those years they didn't perform all kinds of tests after death. The Coroner did a quick autopsy and determined that my dad's neck was broken and that, in his opinion, was all that needed to be determined. The rest I'll never know.

My father was a big man, standing 6' 1" and weighing 225 pounds. His complexion was reddish brown and his hair was poker straight. In contrast, my mother is 5' 3" with a petite frame and a fair complexion, but I learned over the years that, in her own way, she was every bit as tough as my dad!

My father served time in the U. S. Navy during the Korean War. I remember seeing a picture of him and my mother right after he returned from Korea. He was about twenty and my mother was about seventeen. He was wearing his Navy uniform and the picture reminded me of a dream couple. Too bad the dream turned into a nightmare.

We were hurt when we heard the terrible news of my father's death, but not in the same way we would have been if we had lost a loving, caring father. It was more like we were hurt because we had lost him already and he had never really loved us the way it was supposed to be. None of us children would ever experience the fulfillment of having a loving, caring father. He was gone forever.

It is a sad thing for an eleven-year-old boy to never be able to use the word "dad" again. I haven't been able to call a man dad for forty years and it still hurts to this day!

It's a God-given responsibility for every man (father) to be the spiritual leader of his family—to know the Bible for himself and then impart it to his wife and children. In Proverbs, Solomon writes, "Train up a child in the way he should go, and when he is old he will not depart from it" (Proverbs 22:6). The father is the head of the family and directly responsible to God to teach his family about God. But my dad reached for the bottle instead of the Bible.

I can't change how my dad treated me when I was a child, but I do have a choice as to how I will treat my children and so do you. We can all think back about the good times as well as the bad times, even as young as five or six. Small children remember things you say and especially what you do. It's up to each of us, as parents, to train up our children in the way of the Lord. Children are innocent and trusting. Everything we say and do will have an important impact on them for the rest of their lives. Everything!

We're born with a deep need and love for our parents, just as our children are born with a deep need and love for us. Forty years have passed since my dad was killed. And even though he had many shortcomings, I still miss him, I still love him and I still need him!

As long as I can remember we had been poor, but no matter what kind of situation we were in, my mother always made do. At one time, before my father died, we lived in a small second-floor apartment. Actually, it was a cracker box for a family of six. There was no refrigerator and we could not afford one, so my mother had dad nail a wooden produce crate on the outside of our window which faced the alley. It was winter so my mother put perishables such as butter, eggs and milk outside in the crate to keep them from spoiling.

We couldn't always afford toothpaste so my mother would burn bread and scrape the black ashes onto a plate. We would put the ashes on our toothbrushes to clean our teeth. Actually, it worked quite well.

After my dad died, my two sisters, Sharon and Shirley, went to live with my aunt and uncle in Alabama while my mother, brother and I moved in with my grandmother (my mother's mother) in the low-income housing projects in Granite City, Illinois, called Kirkpatrick Homes.

At the time I didn't know it, but as I grew older I realized most of the people in town considered everyone who lived in the projects as "poor white trash." I think our combined rent and utilities were about

$12 a month. Kirkpatrick Homes had many nicknames, but "Passion Flats" was one of the nicer ones.

The projects were two-story buildings laid out in a rectangle. I'm guessing that there must have been forty or fifty buildings in all. Every building was similar. We were bordered on two sides by city streets, one side by a six-foot fence that separated us from the backyards of a row of houses, and the backside was up against an old, abandoned graveyard.

In the summer months the graveyard had weeds six to eight feet high and, of course, it was a favorite place for the project kids to play. The kids from the projects were pretty wild and rebellious. Fighting, stealing, smoking, and drinking were commonplace for the teens.

The graveyard had many trails and secret hideaways that were known only to the people from the projects. Many nights you would see the lights from police cars as they chased someone as far as the graveyard, but that was as far as they went. The cops never went into the graveyard. I even heard that secret gangs met there and animal sacrifices were made there.

The people in the projects were very destructive. There were areas that had wooden benches set in concrete. These benches were carved with graffiti and broken. Some of the brick buildings had filth written on them. Between the rows of brick buildings were concrete alleyways. The project kids roamed the alleys looking for things to do. There were many tough guys in the projects. Many of them are now either in prison for life for murder or have been murdered themselves.

There were two asphalt playgrounds surrounded by fences in the projects. The fences were torn down and only the poles remained. The only part left to play on was the welded monkey bars. All the swings had been busted and single chains hung limp where the seats used to be.

Many times I would hear my mother and grandmother talking in the morning about some woman who had been beat up by her boyfriend or about somebody getting stabbed or shot the night before in the projects. Because every building looked the same, many men came home so drunk that they tried to get into the wrong door. You always locked your doors in the projects because you never knew who was going to try to get in.

During the school summer vacation of my twelfth year something happened that was to change my life forever, although it would not be evident for thirty years.

I was playing basketball at the project court (parking lot with a basket) when a friend came up to me and said, "Danny, there's a man driving through the projects in a church bus asking kids to go a church revival tonight." I said, "What is a revival?" He said, "I don't know, but I'm going." I said, "Okay, me too." Now at twelve years old, with little prior religious upbringing, I wasn't crazy about going to church, but I did think a ride on the church bus would be cool.

That night I went downtown to City Temple Church. City Temple was no ordinary church. It was formerly a movie theater. It was the old style theater, not like today's cinemas. Instead of being a cluster of long, thin rectangular rooms showing a wide selection of movies as the modern cinemas do, this place was awesome in size and had a full balcony. Even the ceiling must have been fifty or sixty feet high.

When my friend and I entered the church building, there was an usher to seat us. Actually he was a deacon, but not having much prior church experience, I didn't know any better.

I remember that the atmosphere was electrifying. There were about 1,000 people singing and praising the Lord. This was like a Monday or Tuesday. I'd never seen anything like this before. I began to feel a presence there that night that I had never felt before.

Later that night, as I lay in my top bunk above my brother David, all I could think about was church and the presence that I felt there. The ride on the church bus was no longer of any importance to me. The next night I went back to City Temple Church and at the end of the service there was an altar call. I went to the altar and I gave my life to Jesus Christ. That night I fell in love with God. I had a peace that I had never had before and I realized that I was happier than I had ever been in my life. I became a walking talking Jesus machine. If you knew me, you heard about Jesus.

For the rest of the summer I went to the church revival almost every night. Can you imagine a twelve-year-old boy on his school summer vacation going to church practically every night when he could have been playing ball, swimming, or camping instead?

Someone in my family gave me a Bible. They thought I was going to be a preacher, but I didn't read it or study it. As a matter of fact, I didn't even go to Bible studies or Sunday school. Instead, I preferred to sit spellbound night after night at the revival listening to the evangelists thunder out powerful messages about salvation and damnation.

A few years earlier, while my father was still alive, I was involved in a serious accident. We were visiting my dad's sister's family in a small rural farm town. It was early in the morning and my dad, my uncle, my brother, and all my older cousins were preparing to go hunting. I was outside throwing rocks at a stop sign near them. As they were loading their guns, one discharged and one of the pellets from a shotgun shell hit the stop sign and ricocheted into the center of my right eye.

At first I thought that a piece of chipped rock had bounced off the stop sign and hit me. I put my hand to my face and blood began streaming down my arms. I screamed for my dad and he ran to me and placed his handkerchief against my eye to stop the bleeding.

By this time everybody was outside and when my mother saw the blood soaked handkerchief held against my face she fainted. Soon after that, they drove me to the nearest hospital. When they laid me on the operating table and took the handkerchief off, everything looked cloudy. They said there was nothing they could do and that I needed a specialist.

We left there and my dad drove as fast as he could to a big hospital in Alton, Illinois. I had lost so much blood on the way that when I got there I was so weak I threw up and passed out. I woke up some forty-eight hours later in a room with several other kids.

A week later they took the bandages off and I could see perfectly. But day by day cataracts began to form and gradually my vision worsened to 20-400. Legally blind. I had lost the vision in my right eye, but if the pellet had been one inch to the left or to the right, I could have been killed.

One night the church was having a Healing Meeting. My brother kept pushing me to go up and get healed, but I was scared. He made such a scene that someone asked him what was going on and he told them about me. I was so embarrassed, but they insisted I go up on stage and let them lay hands on me. I admit, at that time, my brother had more faith than I did that I would be healed. That night my lack of faith kept me from receiving God's healing power. I thought my injury was too much even for God to handle.

City Temple was open twenty-four hours a day. They never locked their doors. I remember one day when I didn't go to school, I went to the church in the afternoon. I was alone and I went up to the altar. The church was very quiet and I didn't detect anyone else in the building. As I knelt at the altar, I reflected in my heart the awesomeness of our God. I had come to love the Lord so much that I wanted to spend quality time with Him even in the afternoon of a school day.

At the end of my summer school vacation I started Junior High. From the first day, I realized there would be temptations in Junior High that I had never faced before.

There were girls in seventh grade. These same female creatures who, just three months prior in sixth grade had pigtails and cooties, were now wearing dresses, makeup, and jewelry. Who would have thought it? Three months ago I wanted to beat them up, but now I wanted to kiss them. Is God good or what?

Then, because I had made the basketball team, I became popular and was invited to all the parties. I began to go to church less and less and school activities and parties more and more. Soon being popular was more important than church, so I stopped going to church altogether.

It was evident that even though I had gone to church all summer long, I had not laid a foundation for my faith. I didn't read the Bible or study it all the time that I had spent in church, and this would prove to be the biggest mistake I had ever made in my life.

I didn't realize it then, but I was already running from God. I was already selling myself out to being a "big man on campus." I began to think being "cool" was the only thing that mattered. I thank God that He is faithful to us even when we are unfaithful to Him. "Now these are the ones sown among thorns; they are the ones who hear the word, and the cares of this world, the deceitfulness of riches, and the desires for other things entering in choke the word, and it becomes unfruitful" (Mark 4:18-19).

The biggest majority of the families in the projects were divorced, unwed mothers, or widowed with children—women who had little or no income who qualified for government assistance. The point is, there were very few children in the projects who had a father living with them.

Most people in town were afraid to even drive through the projects, but one man did and as a result of his courage, a seed was planted in my heart that would eventually change my life forever. To this day, I have no idea who the man driving the church bus was, but God knows. And I'm sure he doesn't remember the skinny little twelve-year-old kid who was more interested in riding on a church bus than in learning about God.

In my early years of High School, I was slapped in the face with the ugly reality of prejudice. I went to pick up a girl with whom I had a date. She invited me to meet her parents. While she was still getting ready, her father and I exchanged small talk. I'll never forget the look on his face when he asked me where I lived and I told him Kirkpatrick Homes.

It never really crossed my mind that I was any different than other boys my age, but the look on his face told me that I wasn't good enough for his daughter—all because of where I was from. That look was worth a thousand words. I was ashamed.

This incident caused a deep emotional wound that began to produce an inner drive never to be poor again, to have things like other people, to be looked up to instead of down on. I never wanted to feel that shame again no matter what I had to do!

My grades in high school were good, but I didn't even try to develop my potential. Most of my efforts to get good grades centered on the fact that I had to have decent grades to continue in varsity sports. However, I still graduated in the top third of my class of 735 with five varsity letters to my credit.

I started drinking the night of my high school graduation party (1966). Our families had a party for my cousin, my best friend, and me. When we walked in wearing our caps and gowns, everybody started cheering and handed us cold beer and toasted us. Someone said, "You're a man now so drink up." Sure, I was eighteen and a man now so it was time I learned how to carry my liquor like a real man.

We were in the middle of the Vietnam war at this time and young men were doing anything and everything to avoid passing the physical for the draft. A guy I knew actually ate day and night until he gained fifty pounds over the accepted weight for his height. Another guy I knew shot himself in the foot with a hunting rifle the day before he was to take his physical.

But me, no way, I was a top-notch physical specimen. I had just graduated from high school with varsity letters in basketball and track. No doubt I was as scared as anyone else to go to Vietnam, but I wasn't about to shoot myself in the foot!

We frequently saw guys in the local newspapers that we had known all of our lives who had been killed just months after they were drafted, some in firefights and some from land mines. One friend from high school came home in a wheelchair and remains there to this day.

Testing for the draft was an all-day affair. There were written tests as well as physical exams. After a full day of testing, I was down to my last test. I was told by an officer to report to the eye exam station. I sat in front of a machine that had an apparatus that looked like binoculars on the front.

The officer told me to put my face against the lens. There was a dark screen with five numbered white round circles side by side in the center. I was told to pick out the number of the circle that was sticking out further than the other four. I couldn't believe it. I couldn't pick out the one. They all looked the same to me. At first the officer thought I was faking so I would fail the exam hoping to be disqualified for the draft.

Then the officer took me aside and shined a light in my eyes. He left and I saw him go over to a panel of officers who were reviewing the finished physicals to give each man his draft rating. He came back over to me and told me to step over to the table of officers. They put a draft card in front of me and stamped it 1-Y, not fit for military service. The injury to my right eye when I was a young boy had caused me to lose my peripheral vision as well as my sight. *Had the accident to my eye as a boy actually caused my life to be spared as a young man?*

At eighteen I moved away from home and decided to put myself through college. I started college the same year that I graduated from high school, but my heart wasn't in it. I attended because it seemed like the right thing to do. I was definitely looking for something, but I couldn't put my finger on it. Something was missing from my life and nothing seemed to satisfy me. Working and putting myself through college wasn't an easy task. Many days found me standing on the side of the road with my books in my hand hitchhiking to school.

These were also the years of flower power, tie-dyed t-shirts, bell bottom pants, and hippies. A whole underground culture began to take root. Many of my friends came back from Vietnam hooked on heroin and hashish. Women were burning their bras in the streets. Men were letting their hair grow long and so did I. I began to identify myself with the "long hairs." I let my hair grow down to my shoulders and started smoking marijuana. I wasn't especially fond of pot, but everyone seemed to be smoking it so I did too. I needed to find myself and this was the way, or so I thought.

I had selected a business major in school and was slowly working my way towards a degree, but then I dropped out and got a job in a local steel mill so I could eat regular meals again for a while.

When I went back to school, I found that everyone was now doing LSD, uppers and downers, along with marijuana. I tried them all at least once, but these didn't help me find myself either. At this time I didn't even know what cocaine was, but I was going to find out soon enough.

I met a special girl in college and we had a daughter out of wedlock. Shortly after our daughter, Stephanie Dawn, was born, her mother decided to marry another man even though I had asked her to marry me. She took our daughter away to another state and it would be years before I was allowed to know her.

After another year of business classes I decided I knew enough to start my own business. I was ready to make it rich. No more hitchhiking and living in trailers with four or five guys for me! I was going to be somebody. I was going to be respected by people like the man who did not think I was good enough for his daughter because I was from the projects.

Taking the world by storm was not as easy as I perceived it to be, but nothing was going to stop me. I took a job with a traveling band as their road manager. We traveled all around the country putting on concerts. It was a lot of driving and late nights in nightclubs, but I was into the party scene so for the time being it was okay. Besides, why should I go through four years of college like those other fools when I could do it faster my way? I could cut the corners and be just as successful as they were. Who needs to follow the rules anyway?

By the time I was twenty-six, I was itching to open a business. I thought about a bar. I should be able to run a bar from my firsthand experience of hanging around in them practically every night. One thing for sure is that they must make money, judging from the amount of my paycheck they got every week!

I knew that I had to come up with something unique. There were bars everywhere so I had to be different. I decided that there were not any bars around for people like me with long hair. I felt uncomfortable going into bars where the parking lot was full of pickup trucks. These were commonly known as redneck bars. No, I wanted a bar where the hippies could feel welcome and I could get their money. I wanted a monopoly on this crowd. I also knew that most of these people were not troublemakers.

For some time I had my eye on a little neighborhood bar on the main drag in town just a few blocks from where I lived. I called the realtor and met with him at the bar. It was old and had been closed for about six months, but it had all the beer boxes and freezers that were needed to start a new business. It was small, but perfect for my first business. I didn't have good enough credit for a bank mortgage, but the owner agreed to carry the paper. I remember the mortgage payment was going to be $250 a month and I was a little afraid that I might not be able to handle such an obligation.

I decided I needed partners because this was too much for me to take on alone. It would take $15,000 to secure the loan, fix up the place and stock the bar to start the business. I could come up with $5,000, but I needed two partners to come up with $5,000 each. Soon, my life long friend John Skubish and his friend John O'Donnell were my new partners. We hired a lawyer, got the liquor license, and planned an opening date.

We took the city by storm. From the first day we opened our doors, we were packed and there were waiting lines halfway down the block practically every night. We made money hand over fist. Within two years after we were open, disco hit the scene. Our little 40 foot x 80 foot bar wasn't big enough to dance in so we bought the house next door and tore it down. We built a wing onto the existing bar and turned it into a neighborhood discotheque. Once again the place was packed. We did all of our construction and changes without borrowing a penny. We paid for everything with cash in the next two years.

During this time I was hungry for more. I was making great money and partying all the time, but something was missing. I thought I needed another business. So I started looking around and found a storefront downtown that would make a great fitness center. I got in touch with a lifelong friend and we decided to go into business together and open a fitness center. Things began to go well there, so now I owned and ran two businesses.

Still there was something missing, so I bought another home with an in-ground pool and two fireplaces. That should make a twenty-eight-year-old man from the projects feel happy and contented. Right? I decided to open a used car lot, then an auto body shop, then a wrecker service and then I bought two motor home recreational vehicles and rented them through my auto body shop. With all my businesses and two homes I must be at least close to being happy now. Right? But I wasn't.

I was prospering in material things. I had money, power, drugs, and women. I partied in limos, private planes, ocean cruises, and on private yachts. I had it going on! I was a self-made man. I was doing my own thing. I made my own rules. But even with all that I had, there was still something missing. I still was not truly happy.

Believe me, I looked everywhere for happiness. The drugs, the booze, and the parties were just temporary thrills that always wore off by the next morning.

I started doing cocaine when I was about thirty years old. I still remember the first time I snorted cocaine. A man came into my office at the discotheque. He put four lines on the desktop. Two lines for him and two for me. I didn't know what cocaine was at first. He said, "Try it. You will like it." I tried it and he was right, I did like it. I said, "How much do I owe you?" He said, "Don't worry about it. It's free." Four years later this man got so high and paranoid one night that he put a pistol to his heart and blew himself away. He wasn't even thirty years old.

After the free sample I started doing cocaine on a daily basis. It seemed to fit in perfectly with the parties and the late night hours. At that time cocaine cost $100 a gram and I was doing about a gram a day. Some for myself and some for my friends. After spending $700 a week for a while, I began to think that there had to be a better way to have my cocaine and keep my money too. I decided to buy cocaine in bulk for a cheaper price, sell most of it and then get what I needed for myself for free. Now that made good sense. After all, I wasn't doing anything wrong. It was just consenting adults having fun with a recreational drug. Right? I bought this lie straight from hell, and without any more thought I became a drug dealer. I had unconsciously opened another business.

I continued to snort cocaine for the next ten years. I opened bigger businesses and partied harder. My first business obligation on the bar was a $250 monthly mortgage. I knew I had come a long way when I took pen in hand to sign a $1.3 million loan for a 12,000-square-foot nightclub that I was a part of opening. The $250 payment seemed quite small compared to the near $20,000 a month loan payment that I was now obligated to pay.

Then I began to hang around with hard-core cocaine addicts. At first I just partied longer and harder. Then one day two close friends of mine told me they had been smoking crack cocaine. They said it was incredible and I just had to try it with them.

I never was a smoker, but what the heck; I was always in control when I did drugs. I owned them and I could put them down anytime I wanted (another lie straight from hell), so I tried smoking cocaine and I didn't like it. My friends were persistent (misery loves company) and talked me into trying it again by telling me how great it was and I would really like it if I gave it one more try. So I tried it once more and when I did, I was hooked instantly. I wanted it all the time.

I had snorted cocaine for ten years thinking that I wasn't addicted. I always made it to work, sometimes with a hangover, but I always took care of business. Things were different now. All of a sudden the drugs were telling me what to do. I stayed up for three and four days around the clock smoking cocaine. I consumed cases of liquor while I was high without eating any food. I still tried to reason that I was in control, but I was just kidding myself.

My habit with my friends got to be so bad that we were doing an ounce of cocaine (28 grams) every time we partied for three days and that was costing $1,000 a whack!

Not only did it cost a fortune to do so much cocaine, but it cost me severely in my businesses. My pager would go off for days when I was high, but I wouldn't return the calls. Not even from my employees who needed to talk to me concerning my business. I couldn't call back because my mind was too fried.

I remember one time in particular that I had been partying with my friends for days. On the third day we got the courage to go through a drive-through to get some sandwiches. We force-fed ourselves and lit up the pipe again. I took a big hit and all of a sudden I felt like I was losing consciousness. I felt like I was going down so I headed for a spare bedroom and fell to the floor. This was about 7:00 A.M.

I woke up around 8:00 P.M. that night and there was nobody there but me. I looked around and the place was spotless. It was so clean I couldn't tell there had been a three-day party going on there. You couldn't tell that there had ever been a party there before.

It wasn't until several months later that it dawned on me why the place was so clean when I woke up. When I was unconscious, the people with me were afraid that I was going to die. They hadn't cleaned my place as a good gesture. They cleaned it to remove any trace of them being there in case I had overdosed. They were paranoid that I was going to die, and they were too scared that they would get in trouble if they had to take me to the emergency room. So they just cleaned the place and split.

Even with all this happening, I was still in the process of opening another business. On the grand opening day of my new tan salon in St. Louis, Missouri, I was stunned by two Drug Enforcement Agents (DEA) who came in dressed in plain clothes. I thought they were customers, and I tried to sell them a tan package. They flashed their ID's and told me they had to talk to me privately. No matter how much you think this couldn't happen to you, when it does it gives you a sickening feeling. They gave me their card and said, "Call us soon."

As soon as the Drug Enforcement Agents left, I called my lawyer and set up an appointment to see him later that afternoon. I told him the story and he told me to call them from his office. So, I called them and they told me that I had better talk to them soon! I told them to set the time and place. They told me to be at a certain Hardees Restaurant the next day at 1:00 P.M. My lawyer told me to meet him at noon and then go to see them from his office, then come straight back to his office after the meeting.

The next day, I walked into Hardees and got a soda. Then I went into the seating area. It was spooky like a scene from a movie. There were feds at every table and one sitting alone motioned for me to come over to his table. I sat down and he showed me a file of papers concerning me. In the file there were statements of a friend to whom I had allegedly sold four ounces of cocaine on two separate occasions. He had supposedly been wired by these very agents and they claimed it was all on tape recordings. The agent told me that I was in serious trouble for cocaine distribution, but he didn't really want me. He wanted some higher-ups who were very close to me. He told me if I would work with him he would make all the papers in the file go away.

I left Hardees in shock. I drove like a madman to my lawyer's office to tell him what had happened. They were going to arrest me for sales of cocaine if I didn't cooperate with them.

I told my lawyer the amount of cocaine they were going to charge me with, and we looked it up in the federal sentencing guidelines book. The guidelines were 27 to 33 months in prison. My lawyer said, "Can you do this if you have to, Danny?" I said, "Yes." He said, "Then let's fight!"

He called the Drug Enforcement Agents I had just met with and told them I had decided to seek legal counsel and not to cooperate with them and that they were to no longer make any type of contact directly to me. For now on they were to contact him if they wanted to reach me and from that time forward we began to plan for my defense.

Weeks dragged by and I didn't hear anything from them, but I could feel them. Everywhere I went I felt like I was being watched. I was paranoid to go anywhere or do anything. I had heard horror stories about how the feds kick in doors at night. I found myself sleeping over at different locations to try to be sure they didn't know where I was at night. This made it very difficult to sleep. I was paranoid day and night.

Then finally it happened. I was going to work one evening at my new tan salon. I always parked in the back of the tan salon so I could go through the back door. As I turned to go into the salon, I was blocked in by several cars and a four-wheel drive truck. Armed DE Agents jumped out and surrounded me. They read me my rights and flashed an arrest warrant. They handcuffed me and shoved me in one of the cars to take me in. I don't care how many times you see this on TV, you can't imagine the fear that goes through your mind when it happens to you.

They took me to the DEA Headquarters and into a private room. There must have been a dozen agents there at the time. Then the Captain came out and started yelling at me and telling me he was going to give me one more chance to cooperate. He said they really didn't want me, but if I didn't cooperate to get the ones they did want, he was going to come down on me hard.

Then he said, "Take a good look at your arrest warrant." I began to read it and I almost fainted. Now there were charges that would give me ten years to life if convicted. I was forty-two years old and if I got the minimum of ten years, I would be fifty-two when I got out. These people weren't playing games!

I remember he said, "Come on, Cox. Do not be stupid. The days of playing the hero are over. Do you think the people you're protecting would protect you? Not in a thousand years."

I don't know what it was, but I just couldn't cooperate with them. Maybe I had grown up with the thinking that related to the old saying "honor among thieves." I was scared to death, but I just couldn't tell on the people that I thought were my friends.

I was thrown into a cell there at the DEA Headquarters in St. Louis for the night. The next morning I was taken before a magistrate at the federal building downtown St. Louis, Missouri. I was formally arraigned and told I would be extradited to the dreaded St. Clair County Jail in Belleville, Illinois.

It was now Thursday, April 11, 1991, and I remember telling my lawyer to get me a bond hearing the next day, Friday, so I wouldn't have to spend the weekend in St. Clair County. He told me he wouldn't be able to get a hearing until at least Monday. I couldn't believe it. I would have to stay at least four days in a place that was well-known as "Gladiator School." At this time I was 6 foot 1 inch, weighing 200 pounds. with a 32-inch waist and a black belt in Martial Arts, and believe me, I was still scared!

CHAPTER 2

True Happiness Is a Gift

As I was being extradited from St. Louis, Missouri, to St. Clair County Jail in Belleville, Illinois, I began to think back in time to eight years earlier—the time I had first become involved in Martial Arts.

Through mutual friends I met an American Black Belt named Jeff Davis. Jeff and I became good friends and he started coming over to my home to give me private karate lessons. At age thirty-four I began to get very serious about my Martial Arts training. Jeff taught a Chinese style of Martial Arts called Kenpo. I began to take lessons three times a week and practice about two hours almost every day.

After working exclusively on defensive and offensive techniques (responses to hypothetical attacks) for about three months, I was able to earn my first two belt ranks. Then Davis started to press me to begin sparring in the ring. At first I did not want to fight. I guess I just wanted to be a textbook black belt. You know—wear a black belt—but never really have to actually fight. Finally, I realized that I was taking karate to learn how to be a disciplined, skilled fighter and not just to have a certificate on the wall. What good is a title if I can't fight?

At this time I weighed about 165 to 170 pounds. I was in good shape, but I was thin from doing so much cocaine. I was considered a middleweight then. One night, Jeff matched me up with a very tough heavyweight opponent (215 pounds) who was the same belt rank. We were going to fight a five-round bout.

Not only was this guy big and strong, but he had a reputation from his past. I had heard that he was formerly a bodyguard to a big shot in the largest, most organized labor union in the country. One day this man was involved in a car bombing.

He and the big shot labor boss got in a car. When they turned the key to start the car, a bomb went off and blew the car to pieces. The labor boss was killed instantly. The man I was going to fight was blown completely through the passenger side door. When he came to, he was lying on the operating room table. He could hear the doctors talking. They were saying that they thought they were going to have to take one hand off because of the damage. He supposedly said, "If I wake up and my hand is missing, you had better never start your car again either." Then he passed out. When he woke up two days later, his hand was still there!

In the first round the heavyweight made a very good fake to my head and I raised both arms to block. Right behind the fake he landed a bone-crushing right heel to my left side ribs. I went down and then took a standing count. My ribs were killing me. I told Davis (who was also the ring judge at the time) that I thought something was broken. He said, "Get back in there Cox and quit whining!"

I guarantee you one thing, you'll find out what you're made of if you ever have to fight after you have been injured. You have a built-in instinct to protect yourself by running and I was no exception. But I couldn't run. The whole Dojo (karate school) was watching and my honor was at stake!

In karate you use both hands and feet as weapons, but I was hurt bad so I had to keep my left side constantly away from my attacker. This made me only half the fighter I should have been. So now I could use only my right leg and my right arm to block or strike. My opponent knew that I was hurt so he came at me harder than ever. He wanted to take me out in the second round and get it over. I fought like my life depended on it. I blocked and counterattacked as hard as I could. He tried everything to get to me, but he took a beating every time he came in. I fought the smartest fight I had ever fought (mostly out of fear).

I finished the fifth round and we bowed to each other (a strict custom in karate). All the other students cheered after the match was over. It had truly been a war. Jeff raised both of our hands in the air over our heads to signify a draw. The heavyweight had to settle for a tie. That night I gained the nickname "buzzsaw" for the tremendous speed (or possibly fear) that I displayed during the fight.

The next morning I could barely move. I went to the doctor and got an x-ray of my ribs. I had a clean break with a one-fourth inch separation to my bottom rib on my left side. I would have to wait until next year to fight in the Missouri Championships.

The doctor simply taped my ribs and told me to take it easy for a while and let it heal. When I went to my friend Tracey's that night, I saw the heavyweight that I had fought the night before. He told me that he had bruises all over his body from my kicks. I had gained a lot of respect, not only from the other students, but from him as well.

My Sensai (teacher), Jeff Davis, is a National Heavyweight Black Belt Champion. He is a third degree with two degrees in weapons. Davis is a big guy. He is about 6 foot, weighing around 230. He can kick like a mule and is extremely quick for his size. When I first started sparring with Jeff he blacked my left eye. Actually, he had a field day on me. He could hit me anytime he pleased.

By the time I got to green belt it was a whole new story. I had only been beaten on one other occasion in competition. My speed and power had increased with every match. But most of all, I had an uncanny ability to read my opponent. Much of the time I could tell what my opponent was going to do just before he did it. Now when Davis and I sparred it was different. He couldn't hit me just anytime he pleased. As a matter of fact, he had a hard time hitting me.

After years of daily training and tournament fighting, I had finally earned my third degree brown belt. Then one day Jeff told me it was "time." I had proved myself in the ring and in the Dojo. I was always prepared for my tests and made very few errors when I was tested for a rank, and I had spent a lot of time and effort to promote karate in the area.

I am not at liberty to tell you exactly what transpires in the black belt test, but let me say that just the techniques alone (some 250) took two straight hours without rest. Then the forms, some had as many as 200 different moves. Then the ultimate test of fighting. There were two guest black belts as well as my instructor who tested me. They were some of the best St. Louis had to offer. You must be physically, emotionally, and intellectually ready to make it through two to four hours of rigorous testing. After the test, I bowed to my black belt panel of judges and waited with my back turned on my knees for the ruling. I was awarded my black belt the first time that I was tested.

The last two years that I competed I decided to fight in the Budweiser Classic Karate Tournament. I won my weight division both years without losing a match. I was proud of my accomplishments, but now I was facing a different situation—possibly even life and death.

The U.S. Marshals had taken me from the courthouse in St. Louis, Missouri, to the county jail in Belleville, Illinois. Belleville is only three or four miles from the notorious East St. Louis, Illinois, area. In this place there were no rules, no-holds-barred, and no being saved by the bell. I was in St. Clair County Jail, better known as Gladiator School.

I was handcuffed and my hands were chained to my waist so that I couldn't lift my hands more than six inches. My legs were shackled with ankle cuffs and a short chain between them so I could only move in slow, short steps. I was still wearing the jeans and a tie-dyed T-shirt that I was wearing when I was arrested the previous day. This was to be the way I was transported from now on!

When I got to St. Clair County Jail, they took off my chains and put me in a holding cell just across from the guards. The cell smelled terrible. The toilet was overflowing with human waste, and you could see where someone had thrown up. No one had cleaned up the mess. There were all kinds of people there. Bikers, drunks, gang members, and some who couldn't speak English. The beds were metal bunks with no mattresses, and it was so crowded that men were sleeping on the floor.

Soon they called me out of the cell and made me strip. They measured me at 6 foot 1 inch and weighed me at 198 pounds, then had me dress in a bright orange jumpsuit with blue slip-on rubber deck shoes. They put me back into the holding cell and told me they would assign me to a cell in a little while.

I knew I was tough because I had proved it against the best in the area, but I didn't know who I might have to fight or how many if I was forced to stand up for myself. It was a sobering feeling.

I heard the sound of a steel door clang open, and then I could hear the sound of men yelling from a distance. It was my turn to go into the permanent housing area. When the guard closed the steel outer door behind us that led to the holding area, I was in a long corridor. I saw several thick steel doors with letters over them to my right. At the end of the hall there were bars with a steel door. To my left was another set of bars that led to the visiting room area, and then beyond that were the women's housing units. I couldn't see anyone yet, but I knew it would be too soon whenever it was.

The guard led the way as we proceeded to the right down the corridor. We stopped at K-Block. K-Block was a state block (holding cell) for state prisoners. The guard told me that normally state and federal prisoners were held separately, but the federal blocks were full so I was going in the state block. I heard that the state blocks were even more dangerous than the federal blocks.

The guard opened the steel door in the corridor. He used a huge metal key about 8 inches long and one-half inch in diameter. I went in first and he came in behind me. I could hear him lock the door behind us.

There was an open area about ten feet to the inner cell and another door. I noticed that there was an inner cell surrounded by walls. The ceiling was made of solid steel plates welded together and the floor was concrete.

The right wall and back wall of the inner cell were solid steel bars one inch thick. On the left, between the left barred wall and the outer solid steel plate wall, was a five foot walkway. The guards could come in the front door and walk all the way around the inner cell and out the back, or come in the back door and walk around the cell to the front door.

The guards walked this area only when they checked for signs of trouble or when they counted us, which was about every two hours. The barred side and front wall allowed them a full view of everything in the inner cell.

The guard opened the steel barred door to the inner cell and as soon as I walked in he slammed it with a pronouncing clang of steel on steel. I heard the sound of the giant key locking me in captivity and locking freedom out. I looked around and every eye was on me, but no one said a word.

I found out later that when you first come in, everybody thinks you might be a plant, a snitch, so everyone is skeptical of you.

There was a small area in front that was a common area. There were three iron picnic benches set in the concrete floor.

Inside our steel cage was another wall of steel bars about a third of the way back with a steel door. This door led into the sleeping area. In the sleeping area there were five sets of bunk beds on one side and five sets on the other side. Twenty bunks in all. Before I could even get to the sleeping area with my mattress someone yelled out, "There ain't any beds left in here. You have to sleep on the floor out there." I didn't know what to do so I found a small area against the wall and doubled my mattress and sat on it there.

I needed a minute to assess my situation and let these men get used to me. I could feel the stares and silent questions. The TV was on so I acted like I was watching. A thousand thoughts were racing through my mind. I sat there silently while there were arguments over card games and what was going to be next on TV.

Slowly I looked around. I counted eighteen blacks, four Hispanics and six whites. Most of the blacks were visibly divided into gangs. They wore their gang names tattooed on their arms with pride. There were the Metros and the Thundercats. There was constant tension between them, but they had to at least tolerate each other temporarily. I was in shock. What was a nice guy like me doing here with all these losers!

The minutes seemed like hours. There was no clock and there were no windows in the steel trap. Time seemed to stand still!

Some guys were walking around in their underwear and some were in their jumpsuits like me. Underwear was hung everywhere on the bars and ropes made out of ripped up T-shirts. The place smelled like body odor. There were twenty-eight men living in a cell made for twenty men. The living area was approximately 15 feet x 35 feet. There was no place to go and no place to hide. Everything you had was subject to be taken away by the stronger ones. Only the strong survived here.

There were no washers, so if you wanted clean clothes you had to wash them in the sink. What small possessions each person had were guarded closely. You were almost afraid to take a shower and leave your belongings because if someone took something of yours while you were in the shower, you either had to fight to get it back or be considered a punk. Then you were a target for abuse.

I noticed a small video camera up in the corner where it was in position to view the entire cell. Then a black man walked up to a speaker on the wall and said, "Hey, man, we need some toilet paper down here and this is the second time I been askin." The voice said, "We'll get down there when we can." End of conversation!

I had been waiting for some guy to get off the phone for quite some time and when he finally got off, I got up and headed for the phone. Before I could get there, somebody said, "It ain't your turn, man. It's mine." I said, "Okay, who's after you?" Somebody said, "I'm after him." After the last guy spoke up I said, "Then I'm after you."

Finally, it was my turn for the phone. I remember calling my lawyer and telling him to get me out of there. I was cussing like a sailor and complaining like crazy. I was blaming anything and everything but myself. He said that he got a bond hearing for Tuesday. "Tuesday!" I said. "I told you to get one for Monday." He said he tried, but this was as soon as the judge would grant a hearing. I desperately needed to get out of there so I could do some cocaine, drink some whiskey, and think over a strategy.

My mind was reeling and I couldn't focus on anything. After awhile another white guy sat on a picnic bench near me and started talking to me. Now I was paranoid. *Was he a plant? Was he a predator? Why was he talking to me?* I thought these things, but I never said anything.

I found out some of the self-imposed rules of this "jungle." The guys who had been there the longest got everything first. First to shower, first to get their food trays and first to shave at the sink. There were a few exceptions to these rules if you were tough enough or downright crazy enough to take a place from somebody else.

There was a stainless steel shower stall in the common room. And there was a stainless steel sink attached to it on one side and a stainless steel toilet attached to the other side. I don't mean a toilet stall. I mean a toilet bowl completely exposed in our day room common area. No walls, no curtain, no privacy whatsoever. If you had to go, you had to go in front of everyone.

I had needed to go to the toilet for quite some time, but I can tell you that I avoided going until I was in pain. And remember, I was wearing a one-piece jumpsuit. To use the toilet I had to take my jumpsuit off my shoulders and down to my ankles in front of twenty-seven men I had never seen before.

Finally, I forced myself to walk over and get undressed and sit down. I felt so humiliated. So degraded. You cannot imagine the shame I felt.

It was bad enough when someone used the toilet in the evening, but imagine someone using the toilet while you were eating. Remember, the toilet was only a few feet away from one of the iron picnic benches.

That night at 10:00 P.M., I heard the guard say through the speaker on the wall, "Lights out and anybody going back get back now!" All the men with bunks in the sleeping area left the common area and went into the back part of the cell. And in just a few minutes the door going into the sleeping area closed electronically.

That left eight of us to sleep on the floor in the common area until breakfast. Everybody seemed to have a place, so I took a spot under one edge of an iron picnic bench close to the shower. This place was mine now and it was up to me to make sure nobody tried to take it away. It was home, at least until Tuesday.

County jails are territorial. Most guys stick together by race or religion. During the next few days, most of the white guys came over and talked to me. One guy in particular invited me to come by his bunk and see some of his family pictures. You never knew who you were dealing with in jail. There were rapists, thieves, child molesters, drug offenders, predators of all kinds, and murderers, to name a few.

As we looked at the pictures, Jerry Jones slowly began to tell me his story. About six years ago he had been arrested for the murder of a friend. The man had been shot in the head twice and he was the chief suspect.

He was charged with murder and brought to St. Clair County Jail. He was released on a $100,000 bond, of which he had to post $10,000 (ten percent), and he was released pending trial.

While he was out on bond, he came up with a diabolical plan. First, he went through the newspapers of small towns in the surrounding areas. He found the obituary of a man close to his age who had recently died. He went to the courthouse in that town and paid $2 for an original birth certificate.

Then he applied for a new Social Security card to match the name on the birth certificate. Let's say the dead man's name was Harold Griffin. Next, he took one of his utility bills and used white-out on his own name and typed in the new name, Harold Griffin. He made copies of the utility bill until it looked like the original.

He did this because you have to have three valid sources of identification to get a driver's license. Once he had all three forms of identification, he went to the driver's license bureau and told them that he had lost his license. He presented the three required forms of identification and they took Jerry's picture and put it on the new driver's license under the name of Harold Griffin. He was now a new man. He was no longer Jerry Jones but Harold Griffin.

He gathered all his money and headed for California. He jumped bail. He started a new life in California with a new identity. He got a job with a progressive corporation and they paid for him to go to night school while he worked during the day. Eventually he got his college degree.

He told me about a month earlier he was doing something on the loading docks where he worked. He was wearing a short-sleeved shirt because it is usually hot in California. As he was carrying on his work duties, he saw a car with men wearing suits pull up and begin talking with one of the truck drivers who had his truck parked at the docks while it was being unloaded. At the time he didn't think much about it, but he saw the truck driver begin to point at him.

Then the men came over and told him they were the FBI and they would like to talk to him for a moment. He said, "Okay." The feds asked him for identification and ran it on their computer. He checked out clean, but the trucker kept insisting that he had seen Jerry on "America's Most Wanted" the night before in his motel room. He said he was sure his name was Jerry Jones. The trucker said he was sure because of the tattoos on both of Jerry's forearms. They were the same tattoos he saw in the police photographs on TV.

When you're first arrested, the police take pictures of all tattoos, scars, and any distinguishing marks such as a birthmark. When they arrested Jerry for murder, they had taken pictures of his tattoos and when "America's Most Wanted" aired his case, they showed close-ups of Jerry's tattoos. The tattoos were a dead giveaway. They took him down to the FBI Headquarters and ran his fingerprints. Sure enough, he was not Harold Griffin but Jerry Jones.

Jerry was taken into custody immediately and extradited back to Belleville, Illinois, to stand trial for murder. He was being held without bond in the same cell as me.

I kept basically to myself through the weekend, holding my breath until I could get out of that place on Tuesday. Finally, at 5:30 A.M. on Tuesday morning, I was pulled out of my cell and taken back to the holding cell up front. Then I was told to take off my jumpsuit and put my dirty street clothes back on.

I was picked up by the U.S. Marshals, handcuffed, and shackled. I was taken to a holding cell in the basement of the East St. Louis, Illinois, Federal Building to wait until I was called for the bond hearing.

At 10:00 A.M., two different Marshals called out my name. I stepped forward and they unlocked the door and handcuffed me again. They then escorted me up an elevator to the second floor and just outside the courtroom they took the cuffs off and stayed very close as they guided me to a huge table where my lawyer was sitting in the courtroom. There was another table across from us where the prosecutor and the arresting DE Agents were sitting.

My lawyer had asked several friends and some family members to testify on my behalf. I couldn't wait to get this thing over with so I could make bond and get out of that place.

My lawyer called ten witnesses. The witnesses all said that I was a hard worker, nonviolent, trustworthy, and responsible. And in their opinion, if I were given bond, I would be in court at the designated time for my trial.

My confidence was building with every witness. That was the lovable guy that I knew I was. It should only be a matter of time now and I would be out of that stupid place. No doubt the judge would agree from the testimony of my friends and family that I was truly a decent guy.

But then the prosecutor called one of the DE Agents to the witness stand. In seconds my credibility was ferociously attacked. He said I was a danger to the community and a flight risk. He said I had been under surveillance and that it didn't appear that I had a permanent residence, that I had been staying in different locations nightly. He also said I was using an alias, which is consistent with a flight risk. My heart sank. Was this man really talking about me? I couldn't possibly be as bad as he was making me out to be!

Just a few days before I was arrested, I bought a small, voice-activated tape recorder and batteries, to take notes while I was driving. I purchased them at Radio Shack. After the clerk rang up my purchase, he asked me for my name, address, and phone number so I gave him a fictitious name, address, and phone number.

When I was arrested, the DEA found this receipt in my car. While I was sitting in the county jail over the weekend, the feds went to the Radio Shack and found the salesclerk from whom I had made the purchase. They showed the clerk my picture and asked him if he remembered the sale. He told them he remembered the sale and me from the picture. I was the one who filled out the information on the receipt.

The agent said at the hearing that, in his opinion, the receipt showed I was beginning to use alias names and that indicated a flight risk. I was astounded! I was merely trying to avoid having my name and address sold to every sales promotion company in the country. His testimony rested on this one incident and he couldn't provide one other shred of evidence that I had ever used any other name besides my own in any situation.

My lawyer cross-examined the agent. He asked him if he had talked to me in person about two months before my arrest and told me if I didn't cooperate with him that he would arrest me. The agent said, "Yes." Then he asked him if he had surveillance at my workplace. The agent told the court that I had been to work consistently since he had talked to me.

In my opinion my lawyer made a strong case that I was not a flight risk because I had gone to work every day knowing full well I was going to be arrested, but I did not run. And, in fact, I had been arrested at my place of business, not in an attempt to flee prosecution.

After all the witnesses had been called and cross-examined to the satisfaction of both defense and prosecution, it was time for the judge to set my bond.

The judge said, "After hearing arguments from both sides, it is the opinion of this court that Mr. Cox is a flight risk and therefore he is denied bond. A court date will be set no more than seventy days from arraignment preserving Mr. Cox's right to a speedy trial."

Flight risk? Hadn't the judge heard my lawyer cross-examining the DE Agent? I had no prior conviction record. No one was physically hurt. Only consenting adults were involved in this matter. I didn't murder anybody. Even Jerry Jones got a bond set and he was indicted on murder charges. I knew they were coming after me and I didn't run.

Then these words came crashing into my mind, "If you don't cooperate, we're going to come down on you hard!" I was getting my first lesson of many of what that really meant.

I looked at my lawyer and he said, "We'll try again in a couple of weeks." "A couple of weeks!" I said. Then he said, "You have to go now.

The Marshals are waiting." I turned around and there they stood. I walked past my family and friends with a blank look on my face. Some were crying and others looked confused and angry.

On my way back to St. Clair County Jail, my mind was in a blur. Horrible thoughts flew through my mind. *I can't do two more weeks in this zoo. Oh, my God, what if I lose my next bond hearing too? I can't do seventy more days in the Gladiator School. I had survived five days, but who knows what tomorrow might bring?*

That night I was so depressed. I called everybody I knew complaining and seeking sympathy, but even sympathy couldn't bring my spirits up. I was in a world of trouble, that much was now very clear. I was at the end of my rope. I had crashed and now I was burning!

The day after my bond hearing I learned that one of my best friends, Jack Stone, had been arrested on charges unrelated to my case. Jack had just testified on my behalf at the bond hearing yesterday and now he was in jail too. Later that day, I found out he was in a cell just across the hall from me. He was only thirty feet away in J-Block, but he might as well be halfway around the world. I knew he needed a friend as much as I did.

The next day something incredible happened to me. About 5:30 P.M. the guard was handing out mail just outside the steel bars. He yelled out, "Cox." I was surprised. I hadn't even been there a week yet and I didn't think anyone had my address.

I walked up to get a single letter. It was from a person I knew, but not well. Her name was Beverly Filer. She was my daughter's aunt. As a matter of fact, I was surprised she even knew I was there.

As soon as I touched the letter I knew something was different about it. I made my way over to my space against the wall and sat down. I opened the letter and began to read. Beverly got straight to the point, and said, "Danny, God still loves you no matter what you have done." As I held the letter I felt like there was an electric shock running down my arms. Instantly, my eyes began to water and I tried to fight back the tears, but I couldn't. There seemed to be an anointing on the letter I couldn't resist. It was like a veil was ripped off my eyes, and I saw the truth for the first time in thirty years. I saw that I was just as bad or worse than every man in that cell. I was a loser. A drug-addict loser. The ugly truth was there. I just couldn't see it until then. Right there, in the jail cell, surrounded by tough gang members, in my heart I asked God to forgive me.

I was changed in a heartbeat, and I was back to that innocent little twelve-year-old boy who had fallen in love with God at City Temple Church. My desire for cocaine, alcohol, and foul language vanished. Then a thought came to me quickly. About two months before I had been smoking crack around the clock for about four days. No sleep. No food. I drank beer, wine, whiskey, champagne, and tequila for four straight days. When I ran out of crack I was so paranoid I couldn't go to get any more. It's a good thing because I would have probably killed myself on it. And I remember saying, *God, help me. I'm out of control. I can't help myself. I can't do this anymore. Help me, God.* God had answered my prayer. The anointed letter had broken every stronghold that I had invited the devil to put on me. And believe me, the devil can't do anything to you unless you let him. He can't.

Then God gave me a desire for His Word. I had peace again. I began to call everyone and tell them the good news! Many of my friends cried with me as I told them the story.

That was it! I had found what I was searching for my whole life. I realized then that I had indeed looked everywhere, everywhere but UP! I had spent a fortune trying to buy happiness when true happiness cannot be bought. It is simply a gift from God. I was now sure there was no true lasting happiness apart from God.

Those free lines of cocaine that were given to me when I was thirty years old had now cost me my life's earnings. Everything I had gathered for my entire life was gone.

Thirty years had passed since the summer of my twelfth year—the same summer that I had fallen in love with God. Thirty years of darkness and running. And just like the scripture says: "Therefore, whoever hears these sayings of Mine, and does them, I will liken him to a wise man who built his house on the rock: and the rain descended, the floods came, and the winds blew and beat on that house; and it did not fall, for it was founded on the rock. Now everyone who hears these sayings of Mine, and does not do them, will be like a foolish man who builds his house on the sand: and the rains descended, the floods came, and the winds blew and beat on that house; and it fell. And great was its fall (my house)" (Matthew 7:24-27).

CHAPTER 3

Gladiator School

My lawyer was Jim Martin from St. Louis. He is a talented criminal lawyer and a friend. I was very comfortable with Jim and I knew I was in good hands, even though I had been griping and complaining at him for the past week.

The very next morning after the disastrous bond hearing, the guards came in at 5:30 A.M. and yelled out, "Cox! Let's go." *Let's go where?* I thought. Again, I was dressed out in my four-day-old street clothes headed for the federal building. I had no idea why I was going there this time. I asked the Marshals, but they wouldn't tell my anything. Maybe my lawyer had talked the judge into giving me a bond after all. *That must be it*, I thought.

When I arrived at the courtroom, I was relieved to be seated by my lawyer Jim Martin. I looked and sitting on the other side of Jim was my close friend Jack Stone. Jack had also retained Martin as his legal defense. I asked Jim what was happening.

He told me one of our mutual friends was cooperating with prosecution against us. This friend told prosecution that he had told Jim Martin some things in private that he felt were confidential and if used against him, it could be damaging to their prosecution. The prosecution had therefore filed a motion to remove Martin as my counsel as well as Stone's.

Jack had introduced a mutual friend named Butch Conners to Jim Martin sometime back. Butch needed some legal advice concerning a trailer of his that had burned down. This man also was now an unindicted co-conspirator in my case and Jack's case, even though our cases were not related.

Now that Conners was working with the prosecution, they were going to try to prove that it would be a conflict of interest for Martin to represent the defense against prosecution. I couldn't believe it. Not only had I lost my bond hearing but now the government was threatening to take away my defense lawyer. He was the only one I trusted!

The conflict of interest hearing was an all-day affair. Martin examined Conners for hours. Then the prosecution cross-examined him. Then Martin asked the judge if he could take the stand in his own behalf. The judge said that this was highly irregular, but if Mr. Martin felt that his testimony would shed more light on the hearing, he was welcome. They swore him in and he testified for over an hour. He produced compelling testimony that I felt was more than adequate to assure the court there was no conflict of interest in my case or Stone's.

The judge recessed for fifteen minutes and came back with his decision. In his opinion, there was a conflict of interest in my case and Stone's. We were told to get new lawyers or the court would appoint us public defenders before the trial. Again, the feds were flexing their muscle. They knew Martin was a great criminal lawyer and a friend. If they could get him dismissed as my counsel I believe they felt that this may lead to an opportunity to break me in the county jail to cooperate against others that they wanted.

Even though Jack was only a few feet away I couldn't communicate with him. I could tell that he was just as frustrated as I was. They kept us separated when we left to go back to the county jail.

On the way back to St. Clair, my head was spinning. *What now? Who would I call?* I didn't really have any other lawyer in mind. I felt like a lamb in a lion's den. No bond, now no lawyer, but I was still facing ten years to life in prison! The twenty-minute ride back seemed to take forever.

About 1:30 P.M. the next day, the guard came in and called my name. He said, "Bunk and junk, Cox." This was the term that meant to get your mattress and all your belongings and go with him. I gathered my stuff and wondered where I was going now. I knew that whether I liked it or not, I had to go with him wherever he told me to go.

When we were in the corridor the guard told me I was being moved to another block. At the end of the corridor there was a steel bar wall dividing another area. The guard called on his radio and the steel-barred door opened electronically. This section was a federal block. A large section had been built onto the existing state building that was intended for federal detainees only. Right before us was a bulletproof glass cage that one guard occupied as a control center. The cage was built in a way that the guard could see into AA-Block, which is on the left and AB-Block, which is on the right.

I soon found out that even though these blocks were separate from the state area, and funded by the federal government solely for federal detainees, the AB-Block was half state and half federal detainees. And, of course, I was going into AB-Block.

After being in that hellhole K-Block, I was relieved that there was a guard visible to everyone, although I found out in just a few days that this wasn't a total deterrent from trouble.

AB-Block was much larger that K-Block. It had a bigger common area and there was a split level area in the back with ten two-man cells up and ten two-man cells down.

I was assigned an upper cell and I almost fainted when I saw that the cell had a tall, thin window about four inches wide and thirty-six inches high. I could actually see into the street. You can't imagine how important the simple things we take for granted every day of our lives are until they are taken away. Then you would give anything for a simple glimpse out a window even if you know you can't go out.

I was put into a cell with a white man. In the past few days, I had been thrown in with a cultural mix that I had not been accustomed to, so for the time being I felt a little more comfortable.

This block was not full! The block held forty men, but there were still a few bunks open. Remember, the guard told me to go into a state block (overcrowded by eight men) because the federal blocks were full? I discovered later that this is one of the ways the feds try to break you. They put you in a dangerous situation and try to scare you into telling on someone. They are fully aware that they are not authorized to mix federal prisoners in with state prisoners, but they do as they please.

There were no men sleeping on the floor in this place. Instead of having an open dorm style area, there are individual cells that accommodate two men each. The day room was huge compared to the other blocks and there was a small refrigerator and a microwave. The day room was in full view of the control center. There were about five metal picnic benches bolted into the concrete floor.

I put my stuff in my cell and went out on the upper landing and just looked around for a moment. My bunkie (the other guy in my cell) was standing next to me giving me the lowdown on who was who. Then he spied a man further down the rail and said, "Oh, yeah, see that guy over there on the rail? Stay away from him. He's a Bible freak. He's always preaching and talking about God."

I decided to take a short nap because I couldn't sleep well when I was in K-Block due to all the noise in the common area.

When I woke up I went down to the common area to eat. The state trustees were allowed to roll in a food cart with twenty trays on one side and twenty on the other side. Even though there was a tray for everyone, there was usually not enough food on each tray. This could cause a severe problem if you were weak.

There were many predators in St. Clair County Jail and they would take food right off your tray or take your whole tray, guard or no guard. I was very cautious about my food. And even though many times I didn't know what we were eating, I ate it all because that was all there was. You can't just browse the frig anytime you want in jail. Some of the predators would walk up to the weak inmates and take their rolls and biscuits, and those inmates were just too scared to protest.

After my meal I strolled up the stairs and guess who was standing on the upstairs rail? The "Bible freak." Even though I was cautioned to stay away from him, something drew me towards him. I stopped next to him on the rail and didn't say anything at first. Eventually, one of us started some small talk. Then he looked at me and said, "You have just given your life to the Lord, haven't you?" I couldn't believe it. How could he possibly know? We were standing with our hands on the rail not far from each other and he said, "Look at the hair on your arms." I looked and the hair on my arms was standing straight up. "Now look at mine," he said. I looked and sure enough the hair on his arms was standing straight up too. He said, "The Holy Spirit is witnessing to me that you are born again."

We introduced ourselves. His name was Bob White. He had been in and out of state prisons for fifteen years. And now he was a federal prisoner. He told me he had been studying the Bible for more than twenty years. He said he would teach me if I were ready. I told him I was ready.

From that day forward I had a God-given desire to know the Word of God. I didn't care what anyone thought. Bob and I spent hours on end reading and studying the Bible. I felt a peace inside even in the eye of the storm. I realized that not only had the long arm of the law been moving, but the longer arm of the Lord was also moving in my life. It was no accident that I was moved to AB-Block instead of AA-Block. I was exactly where God wanted me to be for the time being. He had provided the teacher and I had provided the time.

The next day brought another surprise. Once again I was taken down to the federal building. Once again I had no idea why. When I got to the courthouse, the Marshals escorted me to the huge table, but this time my lawyer, Jim Martin, wasn't there to comfort me and explain everything. I felt small and helpless.

Soon a young woman sat down next to me at the table. The judge came in and proceeded to tell me that if I couldn't afford a lawyer he would appoint me one, but I would have to sign a waiver to a speedy trial. If not, my trial would be set in three weeks. Three weeks? I was facing ten years to life in federal prison with no lawyer and the judge was talking about trial in just twenty-one more days. My head was spinning and I felt sick to my stomach.

Then the judge said, "I have asked one of our new public defenders, Ms. Peabody, to answer any questions you might have before you make your final decision."

From what I understood, either I had to be ready for trial in three weeks or waive my right to a speedy trial. Ms. Peabody said I really didn't have much of a choice unless I thought I could be ready in three weeks. I felt really uncomfortable about this, but I was being pressed into making a decision without proper time and representation.

Finally, I signed the papers for a waiver. Little did I know what would follow this clever maneuver by the government. I had given away my right to a speedy trial and the government was now going to appoint a public defender to represent me.

After I signed the papers, I was taken back to St. Clair Jail. As I walked by J-Block, where my close friend Jack Stone was being held, my thoughts drifted to him and back to when we had first met.

The first time I had ever seen Jack Stone was in my first business. I was in the process of painting and fixing up the little neighborhood bar on Main street that was soon to be open and called "My Old School." I had run out for some supplies and when I got back, there were two guys sitting at the bar drinking glasses of draft beer. What in the world? We weren't even open for business yet!

We had friends helping us fix up the place and one of them had given Jack and his friend some beer. We had our liquor license, but we were definitely not open to the public yet.

I remember thinking I would hate to have to throw this guy out. Jack had huge arms and chest with a small waist. He looked like he was solid as a rock. His friend was Korean, and even though he was very trim and wiry, I had a feeling there was more to him than met the eye. They were both very quiet. They were just finishing their draft beers and I heard them ask for another.

I went over and explained that I appreciated their business, but we weren't really open to the public yet. Could they come back when we were officially open? Jack was surprisingly polite and said he only lived a block away and he would definitely be back. At the time I didn't know if that was good or bad.

Our Grand Opening came and the place was absolutely packed. You could hardly move for the people, and we were overwhelmed with just trying to tend bar. My two partners, two friends, and I, none of us with any previous bartending experience, we were breaking our backs and still we couldn't keep up. We were running out of all kinds of booze, but the people didn't care. They just ordered something else. The music was so loud I couldn't even hear the orders and the people were screaming for us to turn it up!

In the far back of the bar, we had an area with electronic games such as Pin Ball and Shuffleboard. The place was so packed I couldn't see well in that area, but it looked like the games were full and people were waiting for a turn.

About this time I saw Jack trying to get my attention from the end of the bar. I went down to see what it was. He said, "There are some guys starting trouble back there at the Shuffleboard table. I know you are busy, so I'll take care of it if you want me to." I said, "Thanks, man, I would really appreciate it." Then I went back to trying to fill fifty orders at once.

The next thing I knew I saw Jack escorting two big men with beards out the door and he shut it behind them. He came over and said, "They are gone now. It's cool." I said, "Wait a minute. Would you by any chance check I.D.'s for us for free drinks?" He said, "Sure." He hopped up on the bar right next to the door and started to work.

It didn't take long to find out that Jack Stone was considered to be one of the toughest guys in town, and not without reason. From what I was told he had already whipped some of the toughest guys in town, but he never started fights. He only finished them.

At this time Jack had recently finished a tour in the Army. I found out that when he was in boot camp he finished number one out of a battalion of 500 men for top honors in the physical fitness training. He was the only man in boot camp who got a three-day pass for his achievements. After boot camp he went into the Paratroopers and received Survival Training and left the Army with an honorable discharge as Sergeant Stone.

Jack and I became close friends in no time, and he was hired as full-time security in the bar. He threw out the bad guys and there were plenty of them!

I had come to know many personal feats that Jack had accomplished through the years. He was never one to blow his own horn. He was the strong silent type. Soon after I had first met him, he told me that he had bench-pressed 465 pounds at the body weight of 185 pounds. At that time this would have been a world record. Of course, I was real excited and thought he should get his lift in the record books, but he simply said, "Why?" And that was the end of it.

One time Jack told me he had decided to compete in the arm wrestling championship the following month at Six Flags Over St. Louis. The Missouri State Championship Arm Wrestling Tournament was going to take place there. He also told me not to tell anyone. He wanted me to go with him. He trained for a month to get ready, but he had never competed in professional arm wrestling before.

Jack had dropped weight to a very muscular 165 pounds for the contest. He won four straight matches, and then he was going to have to arm wrestle a former state champion in the semifinals to wrestle for the championship.

Jack got psyched up and went on stage. They were set—then Go! Jack slammed the former champ so hard that he fractured the man's wrist. Then he wrestled for the championship but lost. I can tell you that it was only a lack of technique that kept him from being the champion in his first competition. After it was over, some of the participants came up to him and wanted him to train for next year's competition. He just thanked them and said, "I just wanted to see how I would do and now I am done."

Jack's Korean friend was quite a talented man also. Woo had been a Korean National Champion in Tae Kwon Do at seventeen before he came to the United States. While Jack and I were living together, Woo began giving us karate lessons in my basement. He was an excellent teacher, but I had a difficult time understanding his broken English. So later I began to take lessons from Jeff Davis, but Jack continued to learn from Woo.

One time Jack told me he had learned everything that Woo could teach him, and when they sparred he was careful not to hurt Woo. Wow! Hurt this ex-national champion expert? I had seen Woo in action and he was as quick as lightning. Does this give you any idea of what kind of man I'm talking about? Jack would never accept his black belt. He said it wasn't important. He was the toughest man I have ever met.

I had now known Jack for fifteen years. I was still thinking about Jack when I entered AB-Block. There was quite a stir going on when I got there. I asked what was going on and somebody said that there was a riot in J-Block and somebody was almost killed. J-Block? That was where Jack Stone was! They said there was so much blood in the corridor that the trustees had to use mops and buckets to get it up. I asked if anybody knew who it was that was almost killed, and someone said that his name was Malone or something like that.

Fear struck my heart. Jack and I had been like brothers for about fifteen years. I asked around more, but no one seemed to know what really happened or who was involved.

There is an area in St. Clair County Jail called an infirmary. It was actually two small offices that had medical supplies and instruments. There was a physician's assistant there during the day with a nurse, but there was a doctor there only twice a week. Across the hall from the infirmary were two holding cells.

One guy in particular from my block just happened to be in the holding cell when they brought a man to the infirmary who had been in the fight. When he got back, he told it like this.

He said the man was covered with blood, but he was walking on his own power. The guards were in a frenzy and were talking on the radios. The next thing he knew, the Paramedics ran in with a stretcher and put the guy on it. The guards handcuffed his arms and legs to the stretcher and they rolled him out with the guards to the hospital emergency room. After the crew of people left for the city hospital emergency room, the guards were talking and they mentioned that the man on the stretcher was named Stone.

It was Jack! Nobody knew how bad he was. Only time would tell. I called my mother and asked her to stay in touch with Jack's mother and let me know how he was. I told my friend Bob and we immediately went into prayer. Bob always taught me to pray for everything. No matter how small or how big you should always take it to the Lord in prayer. This was big, real big. There was no doubt that he was fighting for his life at that very moment.

Later, I found out what had happened that terrible day in J-Block. Jack was a quiet person. Very strong and very quiet. The gang members in J-Block were loud and obnoxious, playing the TV full blast and slamming cards all day and all night.

After a few days of this, Jack was ready to go off. He asked the guard to see the Lieutenant. Finally, he was allowed two minutes to see the Lieutenant out in the corridor. He politely asked the Lieutenant if he could be moved to another cell because he might go off if they didn't move him. The Lieutenant told him to get used to it!

J-Block was shaped just like K-Block (the first block that I was in). At one point Jack got up and turned the TV off. Then he turned around and told the loudmouths to get back in the sleeping area. Jack had the kind of voice and look that you knew when he meant business. Even though there were about ten gang members, they all went back in the sleeping area. They knew he was either crazy or the worst man they had ever run into.

The gang members didn't know what to do. For some time there was a stalemate and Jack just sat in the day room in silence.

J-Block was overcrowded too, but in J-Block there were cots in the sleeping area for men who didn't have a regular bunk. The cots had two-inch solid oak poles in them. The gang members got together and pulled out the poles and secretly plotted their next move.

Jack was unaware of their plan. He was actually only trying to get them to move him out of the Rapp Trap. He knew the guards could see the cell on closed circuit TV, but they never came down or said a word. There was no way he could hold out forever, something had to give.

Finally, one gang member ran out and jumped on a picnic bench. Jack knocked him off, but as soon as he did he was attacked from behind by the rest of the gang swinging oak poles as hard as they could. Jack blocked many swings and even knocked down several of them, but they kept coming. The odds were overwhelmingly against him.

They were hitting him in the head, arms, back, and legs. Finally, the guards came and unlocked the outer cell door that leads to the corridor. Then they unlocked the inner cell door, but they wouldn't go in to help Jack. They just stepped back into the corridor. They were afraid to go in.

With two or three gang members still hitting him in the head, Jack walked out of the cell under his own power. They couldn't knock him unconscious, but they did rip his head wide open in several places. By the time he got to the corridor, blood was gushing out of his open wounds onto the floor.

His shoulders, arms, and back were covered with blood bruises from the pulverizing blows from the oak poles. He suffered a severe concussion and was immediately put in intensive care at the hospital. It took over a hundred stitches to close the deep cuts in his head. All I could do now was to wait and pray.

In the meantime, I attended church and Bible studies several nights a week as well as private Bible lessons with Bob White. I was puzzled how a man of God could fall from grace so many times. How could Bob break the law again after he had already done fifteen years spread out between two or three different incarcerations? He, like myself, had let himself get hooked on crack cocaine. And once the evil grip of drugs was in place, there was no way he could escape on his own. His addiction led him to jail just like me. He wasn't bitter, but he was ashamed and lonely. Bob didn't have any family. I was sort of his family. I told him about everybody who came to visit me and what my friends said on the phone and at visits.

Once I knew I was going to have to be there at least two more weeks I had a few dollars sent in and bought some items from the jail commissary (a store that offered limited food and hygiene items). It was much easier to guard your possessions in a private cell and with only one cellmate. If for any reason you were pulled out of the cell for court or a visit, your celly could watch your stuff and you could watch his when he was out.

There was no such thing as "contact" visits there. A contact visit occurs when you are in the same room with your visitors. All visits were by telephone through a glass wall. Visiting was two days a week for about fifteen to thirty minutes. I can't tell you any better than that because we never knew for sure. Sometimes it depended on how many other guys in your block were visiting that day, and at other times I think it depended on what mood the guard was in.

There is a long thin room with a one-inch thick bulletproof plate glass separating inmate from visitor. There is also a small divider between each phone and a small stool to sit on while you are talking. We were brought in from the jail side and the visitors were brought in from the street side. The guard's desk was at one end of the phone room.

Sometimes I could visit with three or four different people for five minutes each. I was truly blessed with visitors. Each visitor's day I had at least one visitor. I'll never forget how important those visits were. I lived for them, and I thank God for every visit and every minute they took out of their busy schedules for me.

There were about twelve phones, but you couldn't hear well on all of them. Sometimes guys got mad and slammed them on the countertop and broke them. When they did, it might be weeks before they were repaired.

About a week after I signed the speedy trial waiver, I was assigned a public defender. I was waiting for him one afternoon when I was pulled out of my cell. I went down the corridor with the guard and when we got to the area that led to the rooms for attorney meetings, the guard made me get against the wall so he could frisk me, which was standard procedure every time you had any kind of professional visit.

Then I was taken into a private glassed attorney room just across from control. The guards keep visual contact, but they supposedly can't hear your conversations. I have always wondered if the visits were truly confidential. Why would they record every phone call while you visited and then let you have a private conversation?

I was waiting in the attorney's room when the guard opened the door and said, "Your private investigator will be here in just a moment." Private investigator? I didn't hire any private investigator!

In a few minutes the guard opened the door again, and looking to his left, he said, "Take all the time you want." And who walked in but my mother. I couldn't believe it. I knew that she had taken some tests, of some sort, to do some security work, but a private investigator?

The guard shut the door and we hugged so hard. Tears were streaming down our cheeks. This was the first time since my arrest that I had contact with anyone. We both cried happy tears for a few minutes and then she began to tell me the story of how she was authorized to visit me professionally. A few years prior she developed an interest in doing some investigative work. She enrolled in some courses at a local university. She took special courses in criminology that were required for this field. Then she was required, after receiving certificates from the criminology courses, to take these certificates to be registered to take a firearms test. She passed all the required tests for high velocity handguns.

Then she took this information to the state capitol where she was given a picture identification card that qualified her to be an independent private investigator. All licensed investigators had the privilege of open visits anytime. I was now my mother's first client (non-gratis). She had been cleared by the St. Clair County Chief Administrator and could visit anytime she wanted.

I never heard my mother say one bad word about my incarceration, or ever act like she loved me less for this horrible insult and embarrassment that I had caused her. She was behind me 100 percent. She has never been anything but tireless in her efforts to help me legally, spiritually, and financially. I thank God for mothers everywhere and their prayers.

After that first visit she came to see me often. Many times she wouldn't visit on my regular days so I could spend what little time I was allowed with friends and other family. During her visits she also brought me some clean clothes. I now had appropriate clothes to wear in court.

After I met my new attorney we began to plan for another bond hearing. I was definitely a different person. My whole attitude had changed and my old ways were slowly disappearing. The more I read the Bible, the more my desires changed. It wasn't going to happen overnight, but I can tell you that my friends knew that I was different. I hadn't said one curse word since that day in K-Block, not one. I had no desire or even temptation to do so.

Soon after my mother began to visit as my new investigator, she found out that Jack was going to be okay and that was great news. She also found out that he had been moved to a different county jail and she was in the process of getting cleared to see him there. She was able to visit with Jack one time before he was transferred to Springfield, Missouri, Federal Medical Penitentiary. I didn't know what was happening to him, but I was hoping my mother would be able to keep me informed.

I had been arrested on April 10, 1991, and I was denied bond on April 16th. At that time my first lawyer, Jim Martin, told me that we would try again in two weeks. I didn't think I could do two more weeks in that rat hole, but now my new bond hearing date was scheduled for May 16th and I was very thankful. I had learned a hard lesson in the short time I had been there.

I practically held my breath waiting for May 16th. My new lawyer had been to see me several times and I felt comfortable with him. He seemed pretty sharp. He was close to my age and we got along well. The new peace that I had found through God gave me patience to face the circumstances I was up against.

One thing was for sure; no matter how big, strong, or bad you are, or think you are, there is always someone or something worse than you. Jails are full of the toughest and most evil people you can ever imagine. They can make a deadly weapon in minutes out of just about anything. They form gangs and there is even more power in numbers. You can be beat to death or sexually violated so bad you wish you were dead.

If you are breaking the law right now with drugs or any other crime, consider all that I have said because you are headed straight for a "Gladiator School" near you. A place like St. Clair County Jail can change your life forever in just one day!

CHAPTER 4

Innocent Until Proven Guilty?

As I waited for my second bond hearing, several of my friends began to send me spiritual books. I wasn't accustomed to reading books that had spiritual context, but I loved them now and I couldn't read enough of them. One book in particular was *Good Morning Holy Spirit* by Benny Hinn.[1] I will never forget what Benny Hinn had to say about Kathryn Kuhlman:

While Benny Hinn was attending high school in Toronto, Canada, the minister of the church he was attending asked him to go to a meeting of a healing evangelist, Kathryn Kuhlman, in Pittsburgh, Pennsylvania. Benny knew very little about her except he had seen her on television and she totally turned him off. But the minister was his friend and he didn't want to let him down.

They left Toronto on a seven-hour bus trip to Pittsburgh, but a sudden snowstorm caused them to not reach their motel until one o'clock in the morning. Benny's friend told him they had to get up at five because if they didn't get to the doors of the building before six in the morning, they would never get a seat.

He couldn't believe it. Whoever heard of standing in the freezing cold before sunrise to go to church?

---

[1]   Benny Hinn, *Good Morning Holy Spirit* (Walker & Co., 1991), 2-11,55.

It was bitter cold and still dark when they arrived at the First Presbyterian Church in Pittsburgh. To Benny's surprise, hundreds of people were already in line and the door wouldn't be open for another two hours. There were even people sleeping on the steps. A woman told them it was like that every week.

Finally, the doors opened and they went in and got as close as possible. The place was packed and the gospel music began to play. The people were singing and praying all over with raised hands. Then Benny began to weep. He didn't know why, he just wept. It was a sweet, deep weeping from way down in his soul. It felt as if waves of joy were sweeping over him, but the joy was so incredible that it made him weep.

Then Kathryn Kuhlman appeared on stage. He said he had never felt anything like it before. The presence of the Holy Spirit was so thick in the church that he was almost breathless. He didn't know what she had, but he wanted it with all of his heart.

Once in New York City, Kathryn Kuhlman had just finished preaching at a Full Gospel Businessmen's Convention. She was taken through the kitchen to an elevator to avoid the crowd. The cooks had no idea a meeting was going on and had never heard of Miss Kuhlman. In their white hats and aprons, the cooks didn't even know she was walking by, and the next thing you know they were flat on the floor. Why? Kathryn didn't pray for them, she just walked. What happened? When she left the meeting, it seemed as though the power of the Holy Spirit attended her! Who is the Holy Spirit? The power of the Lord!

His minister had told him about the miracles that took place in Miss Kuhlman's meetings, but he had no idea what he was about to witness in the next three hours. People who had been deaf suddenly could hear. A woman got up out of her wheelchair. There were testimonies of healings for tumors, arthritis, headaches, and more. Even her severest critics have acknowledged the genuine healings that took place in her meetings.

He saw many miracles of healing that day and he never forgot who she was. As I read the book, I knew I could never forget Kathryn Kuhlman either.

Spirit inspired, I focused on God more than anything else, and the next few days, until my second bond hearing, seemed to pass quickly. Finally, the 16th of May had arrived. Now I would get a bond and go home to my family to prepare for my trial. Thank God!

The bond hearing followed the same procedure as the first. My new lawyer, Steve Simmons, called several witnesses on my behalf. These witnesses were once again cross-examined by prosecution. Then came the same DE Agent who caused me to lose my first bond hearing. He presented the same case and then my lawyer had his opportunity to cross-examine. He had done his homework and reviewed the testimony from the first bond hearing, and was ready for their objections.

Upon careful cross-examination of the agent, Simmons made a case in my favor.

The agent said that he had contacted me about two months prior to my arrest. During that contact he had made it perfectly clear to me that if I didn't cooperate with him against others, he would arrest me at an undisclosed future date. He said he was contacted that same day by my previous lawyer, Jim Martin, who told him I didn't wish to cooperate and he was representing me in that matter. The agent was unable to produce any subsequent evidence that I had ever used an alias other than at Radio Shack. He admitted that I had maintained a regular work schedule without any indication of running, and in fact, he picked me up at my business on my way to work.

Simmons brought attention to the court that if I had ever intended to flee prosecution, I had a full two months from the initial contact of the DEA until the time of my arrest to do so.

After a very short recess the judge said that in his opinion I was still a flight risk, that there would be no bond set and I was to be kept in custody until such time as I would be tried in his court of law.

I had heard in so many cases that the judge always grants you a bond the second time and even if you get a bond set so high you cannot possibly match it, in a few weeks he will reduce the amount to something reasonable. Not this time!

I was absolutely devastated. For the first time, the ugly reality set in that I wasn't leaving jail, not unless I was found innocent in trial. I had to go back to St. Clair County Jail again and struggle through lonely, dangerous days and try to prepare for my defense from inside the jail. I already knew from talking to others that lawyers take care of the people who are in their face first. The people who are able to call direct and go to the lawyer's office for convenience. When you are in jail, you must call your lawyer collect. If they are busy or not in, the secretary simply does not accept the call. This is humiliating and frustrating.

I also found that a lawyer may have every intention of coming to see you, but if their day wears on and it gets late, it is usually the ones in jail he will not have time for. Simmons' office is a forty-minute drive to St. Clair County. At first he was right on time and never missed, but as time wore on, things changed. The problem was that if your lawyer couldn't make it, he didn't contact you and tell you he wasn't coming. He just left you hanging, wondering and waiting until it got so late that all visiting hours were over, even for attorneys. Then you knew you were not going to see him!

Time wore on through the end of May and the first part of June. I had a court date sometime in early August. I had developed a urinary problem just before I was arrested and it began to bother me. I told the physician's assistant. He scheduled for me to see a private urologist in the city. I was taken out of St. Clair (in my orange jumpsuit) in chains to a specialist. He examined me and said he would send a full report to the jail, but in his opinion I needed professional care.

My lawyer was able to get a copy of the medical report. We discussed it and he decided to ask for another bond for the purpose of medical treatment. It was worth a try.

Simmons prepared a motion and filed it with the courts asking for the judge to release me on bond for medical treatment. Within a week the judge ruled. He ruled in favor of the medical treatment, but he ruled against a bond for my release. This made three bond denials in a row. Instead, he was going to order that I be sent to prison to get medical attention. Prison? Just the word gave me chills. I hadn't even been tried yet, how could they send me to prison? I thought in this country you were innocent until proven guilty. One thing was obvious. I belonged to the court and whatever the judge ruled I would have to comply with it.

At the end of June, the morning finally came. It was funny how I hated St. Clair County so bad, but I didn't want to go to prison. I'll admit it. I was scared. At least I knew what to expect in St. Clair, but the only thing I knew about prison was what I had seen on TV.

Very early one morning I heard the guard say, "Cox! Bunk and junk." This was it. I had to go. I gathered up my stuff and a few guys wished me well. Bob and I had a short prayer. He was real sad to see me go. Then I was taken to the control center and prepared to ship out to prison.

Five other men and I were chained and shackled and led into a van waiting outside. There were two Marshals assigned to take us to wherever we were going.

At first it was pleasant to see the countryside roll by and see familiar places that I had been before. Then it became painfully sad that I had no idea when I would ever be able to enjoy freedom and these places again. The trip turned into hours and we were all miserable in the chains and we had to go to the bathroom bad.

I didn't know what miserable was until we rolled into the main drive that led up to Terre Haute, Indiana, Federal Penitentiary. Let me tell you that if I didn't know how much trouble I was in, I knew it then.

Terre Haute Penitentiary was a sixty-year-old prison surrounded by two giant fences topped with razor wire. Barbed wire was always used to top fences for maximum security until razor wire was developed. The outdated barbed wire had twisted barbs running along a wire. The new razor wire had actual razor blades running along the wire.

If you made it to the fence without being gunned down, the barbed wire would make it difficult to get over the fence. Now if you made it to the fence and got to the top, the razor wire would slice you to ribbons before you could make it to freedom.

Huge old brick buildings rose up like monsters out of an open field. This place held between 1,500 to 2,000 men at a given time. Two fences surrounded the penitentiary. They were about ten feet high and separated by about fifteen feet. There was an outer fence and an inner fence. In the area between the fences, there were rolls and rolls of razor wire. If you made it over the first fence, you would have to climb over razor wire ten feet high and fifteen feet wide. No one ever escaped.

As we pulled up in the van, the Marshals stopped at a speaker box some distance from the main entrance. They reported in and were given authorization to proceed to the front entrance. It all sounded very serious. As we approached I could see men in bulletproof vests, with mirrored sunglasses and they were carrying shotguns. There was a gun tower right in front of the main entrance. It was a wooden building raised up on what looked like stilts. On the outside of the small building was a wooden catwalk.

Upon exiting the van I looked up and there were more guards with rifles trained on us as we walked. We were told to walk up to a gate that went through the center of the razor wire and stand there until our name was called out. There was a walkway about five feet wide that went straight through the razor wire fences. It looked like a thin cattle run.

I could see prison guards waiting on the inside at a gate at the other end of the cattle run. They opened the outer gate, but the inner gate was still closed. One of the men with a shotgun barked out our names and told us to get our butts in the gate. After all six of us were inside the gate, he shut and locked it. We walked to the far end of the cattle run and another prison guard opened the inner gate.

He told us to step into the yard as he called our names. One by one we stepped forward until all six were inside the inner fence of Terre

Haute, Indiana, Federal Penitentiary. I glanced over my shoulder and all the men with shotguns were still aiming at us. Then the guard shut and locked the inner gate and called to them that all was secure. Then the men on the ground began to unload their weapons, but the men on the catwalk still followed us with rifles. You can't imagine how weak you feel in a situation like this.

We had a long walk across the prison yard and as we neared the area called "Receiving & Discharging" (R&D), we could hear the calls from men inside the cell blocks. Things like, "Hey, new meat—we've been waiting for you." "You with the long blond hair, you're sleeping with me tonight! Hurry up, girls. We are so lonely," etc.

Why was I there? I was supposed to go to a medical prison. There must be some mistake. I didn't belong there with those violent predators. I had been indicted as a first-time nonviolent offender. I hadn't even been tried yet. But for now I didn't want any more trouble than I had already, so I just kept my mouth shut.

We were all put in a long bullpen type cell and told to strip off and give them all our clothes. One by one they started fitting us with new (not new but different) prison clothes. One by one we had to talk to a shrink, then a physician's assistant, then finally a case manager.

Finally, it was my turn to see the case manager. First thing he asked was how much time I got. I said, "None. I haven't even been to trial yet." He said, "What? Then what the hell are you doing here?" I said, "I don't know."

He got on the phone and called someone all frantic and then said, "You get back in the cell in there." I went back and they locked me up by myself. He said, "We'll take care of you in a minute."

I waited like what seemed forever wondering what was going on. Can you imagine? You are nothing in prison. You have no rights to know anything. You are on a "need to know basis," and as far as they are concerned you don't need to know.

After another hour I saw some men in white shirts with badges talking to the case manager. He pointed me out to them. They were holding chains in their hands. They opened my cell door and told me to come with them. I was stripped and searched again. Then they put chains on me again. This was just like the Marshals who transported me here. So now after waiting for twelve hours to get out of chains, I was back in chains again.

The men were county sheriffs. They were taking me to the Terre Haute, Indiana, County Jail. By the time I went through the whole process again, it was about 7:00 P.M. before I got to a bunk. Altogether the two-and-a-half hour ride to Terre Haute, Indiana, turned out to be a twelve-hour nightmare. My hands and ankles were raw from the steel cuffs and I was starving.

The block in Terre Haute was a shotgun type. All the cells were against one wall with bars in front. There were two-man cells and four-man cells. The guys who had been there the longest had the two-man cells so I had to go into a four-man cell.

Everything was solid steel. In the small cell there were two stainless steel bunks welded to the wall on the left and two on the right. In the middle in the back, there was a stainless steel toilet with a tiny water fountain and washbasin. I was given a two-inch thick mattress, a wool blanket, and a pillow. I was so exhausted that I went to bed soon after I arrived. At 9:00 P.M. they made you go into the cells and then closed the barred doors electronically. That was it for the night. You didn't get out until the next morning for breakfast.

There were about twenty men in this block. There was a small walkway beside the individual cells so I decided to lay out in the walkway during the day so I didn't have to be cramped up in that room with three other men.

There were no Bibles to be found. When they brought the food, I asked for one and the guard said he didn't know of any around. I was frustrated. Some of the men there said I would probably be held there until the prison airlift came through Terre Haute the following week. I had already missed the one for that week.

To my surprise the guard that brought our food that evening said, "Who wanted the Bible?" I said, "I do." He handed it through the bars and I began to read. I read the Bible for hours each day. As soon as they opened our cell doors I pulled my mattress out in the walkway and read until nightfall.

On the third day, there were words between two blacks. I never did find out what the problem was, but they started swinging and went at it for quite some time. Neither could knock the other out, but there was blood drawn and one man got busted up pretty bad. That place was a steel trap and the guards couldn't see in or hear anything that was going on. It was dangerous just like St. Clair County. You could get killed and no one would know about it for hours.

I kept my mouth shut and read all day every day. By the time I was told to "bunk and junk," I had read the entire New Testament for the first time in my life. Praise God!

This time the Marshals came to get me again. This would be my first trip flying in the Federal Bureau of Prisons system. I would be flying on "Conair" as the prisoners called it.

When I got to the airport and looked out the back of the Marshal's car, I could see other cars, vans, and buses loaded with prisoners who were going on the Conair also. There would be others who would come off the plane and leave in one of the many vehicles that were waiting.

There were men with bulletproof vests, sunglasses, and rifles standing everywhere. I found that when the plane comes in, the Marshals surround the plane and guard it until it takes off again. The plane always landed and unloaded in a special area that was off limits to the general public. No unauthorized persons could even approach the area while loading and unloading.

As soon as the plane came in and the area was secured by armed guards, the vehicles all pulled up in a semicircle at the back of the plane. The Marshals from the plane came down the back steps (the Conair loaded from the tail by a built-in step that raised and lowered) and so began the process of loading and unloading the prisoners. They talked with the Marshals from each vehicle and determined if their records matched. There were boxes and boxes of records and files that had to go with each prisoner. When the prisoners came off the plane, they were directed to the vehicle that was waiting for them. They were then searched thoroughly before being admitted into the vehicle. When someone got out of a vehicle to go on the plane, the Marshals were waiting from the plane to search them before boarding. It was like a scene from a movie. It was incredible.

One after another the men, and a few women, slowly walked down the back steps in single file. You could hear the sound of chains clanking together as they took each step one at a time. Then it was time to load the plane. I was directed to walk towards a Marshal from the plane. She searched me thoroughly and pointed to the steps. I walked slowly behind the others who were already forming a line up the steps.

There was a Marshal standing in the aisle telling you where to sit. "You here, you there, you up front," and so forth. The plane holds about 120 prisoners in all. The women prisoners were all seated up front away from the male prisoners.

There are three seats on each side of the aisle. The plane is normally packed at every stop. It's very difficult to move in those close quarters when you are all chained up. It's also difficult to use the bathroom. I learned a valuable lesson that day that if I ever had to fly Conair again. I knew I wouldn't eat or drink hours before I flew.

Prisoners were asking to go to the bathroom, but the Marshals said they would let everybody go after they had reached a certain distance and altitude away from the airport.

Finally, they announced that they would let us go row by row. When it was my turn I struggled out of my seat trying not to step on the guy's feet near me and apologizing when I did. As I walked toward the back, I saw one Marshal holding the doors open to a bathroom on each side of the walkway with his feet. You had to go with the doors wide open or you didn't go at all.

I was wearing a t-shirt with khaki pants. They had an elastic band around the waist. My hands were handcuffed together and then hooked to a chain around my waist. I could only move my hands a few inches. It was going to be difficult, but I had to figure out a way to do it.

I spread my feet apart and leaned my forehead against the bathroom wall so I could balance myself while the plane was moving. Then I slowly worked my thumbs under the elastic band on my pants until I could get myself in position. With a monumental effort I finally was able to relieve myself. No matter how careful you were, this compromise was subject to mishaps. You can also use your imagination of what you would have to go through if you had to make a movement.

We stopped at different prisons to drop off and pick up prisoners. About five hours later we were approaching Rochester, Minnesota, Airport. This was the medium-level federal medical prison. I prayed to God that they would not make any mistakes and keep me on the plane. I knew that this was a distinct possibility.

We were unloaded in the same fashion as we were loaded. I was picked up, with about fifteen other men, by a prison bus from Rochester Prison. The bus trip was about twenty minutes. I was still nervous, but I wanted to get where I was going and get the chains off. It had already been ten hours since I started this trip in chains that morning.

Rochester Prison was actually in town. I could see the high school football field on one side and a park on the other and homes on the other. It was much smaller and newer than Terre Haute Penitentiary, but just as menacing with the razor wire fences. As we pulled up to the entrance I could see the guards in bulletproof vests waiting for us. This would be my new home. For how long I didn't know!

I went through the whole process of being booked in through the R&D, then I was assigned a cell. I was taken by the R&D guard to the block that I was assigned. I was then taken by the block guard to my cell and put my stuff, such as prison issued toothpaste and a brush, in my locker.

The guard left and I was on my own. I wasn't locked down there. Prison gave you more freedom in some ways than a county jail. You could move to different places. I wasn't used to this and I was very tentative at first. I had been browbeaten in the county jail for so long that I was even apprehensive about going outside, even though it was permitted here.

Finally, I ventured outside and found an empty bench to sit on. I didn't feel like talking to anybody. I just wanted a few minutes of silence to reflect on the avalanche of events that had taken place in my life over the past three months. It was already July 2nd and this was the first time I had been outside without chains and Marshals in three months.

I sat on the bench and marveled as a huge, orange sun began to set. Tears welled in my eyes as I watched the sun set for the first time in years.

CHAPTER 5

Hospice

As I looked around Rochester Prison I saw several buildings. Each building had a number. I lived in 10-Building, second floor, which would be called 10-2.

The 10-Building housed all prisoners sent there for medical evaluations who didn't have psychological problems. 1-Building housed inmates with psychological problems, plus a special suicide watch unit. 9-Building housed the very sick and terminally ill who needed continual attention from doctors and nurses. 2-Building housed the healthy working inmates, plus a special drug rehabilitation unit and 4-Building also housed the working inmates who were healthy.

The Chapel is located in the middle of the compound, and off to the side of the Chapel was the Education Building. In Education, inmates were schooled to get their G.E.D. Also, the workout area, poolroom, and library are located in the Education Building.

The Dining Hall, better known as "The Chow Hall" (in most all prisons) is located on the front side of 2-Building. The Prison Yard is located on the west side of 10-Building right behind where I was housed. The Yard has a one-eighth mile asphalt jogging track, a basketball court, weight lifting area, two boccie courts, two handball courts, and a softball field.

In the county jail you are locked down twenty-four hours a day in a small block averaging twenty to forty men. You rarely left the area unless you had a specific reason like an attorney visit, family visit, medical attention, or church. And if there were a major disturbance anywhere, at any time, all of these would be canceled. Prisons are totally different. You are able to move about according to what your needs are or to perform your daily work assignment. It's like living in a small self-sufficient city.

There is a guard station on every floor of each housing unit. If you are assigned a job, you are not allowed to be in your unit between 8:00 A.M. and 4:00 P.M. except at lunch. There are five separate counts of the inmates Monday through Friday and six counts on Saturday and Sunday. The counts are at 4 P.M., 9 P.M., 12 A.M., 3 A.M. and 5 A.M. At the four o'clock count, every inmate in the prison system has to stand while they count. Someone said that's so the guards can tell if you're still alive.

We could move about the compound from 8:00 A.M. to 9:00 P.M., but at 9 P.M. each building is locked. I could still move about on my floor to the restroom, showers, TV rooms, and the laundry. I could also visit with other inmates in other cells on my floor until 10:00 P.M. (lights out). No one else is allowed to enter a different housing unit other than your own without direct permission or orders to do so from staff.

Normally, security levels are never mixed. One inmate rated as a maximum security risk, for example, couldn't go to a low security prison and vice versa. Even though I hadn't been to trial yet, I was given a low/in ("in" meaning behind a wall or fence) security rating. There were some inmates there with two-year sentences for writing bad checks as well as lifers for murder and bank robbery. The problem is that you can't tell who is who just by looking at them.

On the wall right next to the guard's office is a bulletin board where all announcements or "callouts" are posted. It's the responsibility of each inmate to check the callouts carefully each evening to see if they are called out the following day by staff to be in a particular place at a particular time. Failure to make a callout resulted in disciplinary action.

The guard explained to me how the callouts worked so I began to check them carefully each evening. Within a few days, I was called out to begin a series of evaluations through medical.

First, I was called out to the Lab. There I gave blood and a urine sample. Then the nurse checked my blood pressure and took my pulse. The following day I was called out to the psychiatrist. Next, I was screened by a physician's assistant (PA). The PA went over my entire medical history with me. He told me that I should watch the callouts for an appointment with an urologist in the near future. Then he asked me if there was anything that I wanted to add. I said, "Well, there is one thing. I was shot in the eye with a shotgun at nine years old, and my right eye is filled with cataracts. My vision is 20-400 in that eye." The PA made a note of it. After that it never crossed my mind.

About a week after I was screened by the PA, I heard my name being called over the PA System to report to the officer station on 10-2. I went there and he told me to get dressed in my full prison khakis and report to the hospital in fifteen minutes. I asked him why and he just said, "Be there."

I got dressed and walked over to the hospital, and when I got there two officers were waiting for me. One took me into a small room and strip-searched me, then told me to get dressed again. After I was dressed, I was told I was going to downtown Rochester to the hospital to see a specialist. That was all they would tell me.

I was to be escorted in handcuffs by two guards to the hospital. When we approached the hospital, I could see that I was going to the

Mayo Clinic. I had heard so much about Mayo, but I never thought I would ever be there, especially like this. I was taken in a side door to a service elevator. We were met there by a Mayo staff member and I was seated in a wheelchair. Then they laid a towel over my cuffed hands so I would be as inconspicuous as possible. I felt really stupid.

When we arrived at the designated floor, I noticed a sign that said "Optometry." I thought I was going to see a urologist. What in the world was I doing on this floor? I was there to see a specialist all right, but the doctor was an eye specialist, not a urologist.

The doctor examined me with an assortment of different machines and lights. She told me she would evaluate the results and get back with me. That was the end of the visit. One week later I was in her office again. This time she told me that I was a perfect candidate for an interoccular lens transplant. She said my cornea was still intact and not damaged from the accident. She had a giant plastic eye that came apart in sections and she carefully explained the process using the plastic eye as an example.

She asked me if I would consider the operation. I told her I would agree to the operation. On the way back to the prison, the guards were saying that there was no way the Warden would approve the operation because it was not life threatening.

I had no say either way so I just went about my business and waited to see what would happen. In the meantime, I got involved in the church as much as possible. I went to Bible studies and church on Sunday. It was incredible to go to a real church, and I found that when I got a visit, my family could attend church with me. I was amazed!

My celly told me he belonged to an inmate volunteer group called Hospice. I had never heard of Hospice before so I asked more about it.

He said the chaplain was in charge of it and they met once a week at the Chapel on Wednesday nights. He told me I should go with him the next meeting. So I did.

I learned that there were about eight to ten inmate volunteers out of a population of approximately 1,000 men. Each man spent time with the very sick and terminally ill in 9-Building. Each inmate had to go through a special training course, then be approved by the chaplain and the Warden. The volunteers did everything from read books and letters to sick inmates to hand feeding the ones who couldn't attend to themselves. I had a strong desire to help in any way I could.

After the meeting I approached the chaplain and asked him about being a volunteer Hospice worker. When he found out that I was pretrial he told me I couldn't be involved in the program. I couldn't understand this since it was all volunteer anyway. I would think they would welcome all the help they could get. I asked him if I could please just continue to sit in on the meetings and take the training anyway. He agreed to that, but reminded me that I wouldn't be able to be a volunteer.

I was called out to the hospital doctor in the next few weeks and he told me I had been approved by the Warden for the interoccular lens transplant. I was overjoyed. Praise God! The Warden had made an exception even though it wasn't something that was done very often. I knew the Lord was walking with me every step of the way.

Within the week I was taken to the Mayo Clinic for the surgery. I was prepped and sent into the surgery room. I was totally awake as the two specialists made a half-circle incision around the upper half of the color of my eye. Then they took out the old lens that was covered with cataracts and put in a new lens made of plastic. They sewed me up with seven stitches and I was on my way back to the prison. Just like that.

When I had recuperated for the proper amount of time, I was taken back to Mayo to be examined. The doctor tested me and I now had 20-40 vision. I had gone from legally blind in my right eye to 20-40. It wasn't perfect, but I could definitely see well enough to drive with the new lens if I had to. Even though I didn't have the faith as a young boy to receive my healing, the Lord gave me the next best thing. He sent me to the Mayo Clinic and let the specialists give me a new plastic transplant and the government paid for it. I went to one of the best hospitals in the world for my surgery and it was free! When God does something, He always goes first class. And this wouldn't be the last time I would fly first class on the wings of God.

After my surgery I went right back to my training in Hospice. Then one night as I sat in on a meeting a wonderful thing happened. One of the inmates told the group that he was getting out in a week or so. Then another volunteer said he was being transferred soon. That left the group seriously shorthanded.

The chaplain tried to double up and stretch the help he had to remedy the situation, but nothing seemed to work. Then he looked at me and a smile crossed my face bigger than the Grand Canyon because I knew the Lord was opening another door that looked like it couldn't be opened.

The chaplain told me he would have to pull some strings, but if I was still interested I would probably start the next day. I was a whole new man. I couldn't wait to serve the Lord through serving my fellow man. I felt humble and in awe of how the Lord blessed my obedience even when I was told I couldn't be a volunteer Hospice worker. Nothing is too big and nothing is too small for the Lord.

My first assignment as a Hospice volunteer was a man named Walter. Walter was quite a colorful character. He had been in prison for over twenty years and he was sixty-seven years old. He had been arrested for a string of bank robberies. He told me that in his last bank robbery he kidnapped the bank president's wife (by consent he says) and held her for ransom. Of course he was caught and sentenced to thirty-five years.

Walter started his prison sentence on the Rock at Alcatraz Prison in California. Then when Alcatraz closed, he was sent to Leavenworth, Kansas, Penitentiary. He was accused of murdering a man there. He was never proven guilty, but he was sent to the Super Maximum Prison in Marion, Illinois, anyway. There he spent three years in a cell by himself, locked down 24-7 for disciplinary purposes.

Walter had Parkinson's disease and a diabetic condition. He was chronically ill. He had a clear mind, but his body shook uncontrollably from the Parkinson's. My duties as a volunteer were to spoon-feed Walter at dinner and write letters for him. Of course, the nurses fed him the other meals of the day, but we volunteers helped out as much as possible when we could.

As I became more familiar to the nurses and doctors in 9-Building they began to use me for more responsibilities. When they knew that I was there because I genuinely wanted to help, they asked me to help with other patients as well as Walter. I was very thankful to help all I could because that's what I volunteered to do—to help others.

I was scheduled to see the urologist, but he came out to the prison hospital instead of me having to go into town. He gave me a thorough examination and decided that he would conduct an exploratory examination of my bladder area for any signs of cancer.

About a week later I was scheduled for an outpatient procedure in the prison hospital. The exploratory exam revealed that my bladder and urinary track were cancer-free, and I was treated for the original problem that had caused my lawyer to file for medical attention. Everything was fine.

After I had been in Rochester for about two months, I was told by my case manager that the judge had rescheduled my trial and I would be released from there back to the county jail soon. I had been spending so much time in 9-Building as a Hospice volunteer I had kind of put the trial in the back of my mind. Or maybe it was the dread I felt in my heart about returning to St. Clair County Jail and facing the charges. Finally, the day came when I was called to R&D. They told me to bring over all my property and they would get me ready to be transferred back to county. I gathered what little I had and gave it to them. Now I was ready to move again.

I had to go back through the system via Conair. I was taken by a twenty-minute bus ride back to the Rochester Airport and then boarded the plane. We stopped first in Sioux Falls, South Dakota, to let prisoners off who would be going to Yankton, South Dakota, Prison. Then back in the air to our next stop.

Little did I know, but I wasn't going straight home like I thought. I was going to El Reno, Oklahoma! Oklahoma City was the last stop for the day. If you were still on the plane when it got to Oklahoma City, you were going to El Reno Prison for the night, or maybe the month. You had no way of knowing.

When we stepped off the plane in Oklahoma City, we were directed onto two huge buses. There were about 120 men in all. The bus ride to El Reno Federal Prison, which had a regional holdover center as well as housing for 2,000 inmates, was about forty-five minutes.

It was about 7:30 P.M. when we pulled up in front of the razor wire fences. As we sat on the buses, we were given sack lunches for dinner. One sandwich with cheese and one sandwich with salami, one Granola bar and one carton of juice. I have never understood the sandwich thing. The first thing everybody did was try to get the cheese and meat on one sandwich. This is extremely hard when your hands are cuffed and chained to your waist. After struggling through our meager meal, we still sat there for another hour. By this time we were all miserable.

Finally, we were all herded into the El Reno Prison under armed guard. I noticed that some men had "black boxes" around their hand-cuffs. I later learned that these boxes were put on men who required top security. The black boxes are so rigid that there is virtually no way to move your wrists at all. These men usually had violent crime sentences or life sentences with a high risk factor of escape.

In El Reno we were separated into two bullpen runs. After another hour still in chains, we saw the guards setting up stations to take our chains off. In front of the bullpens, they set up fifty gallon trash cans to store the handcuffs, leg irons, and waist chains.

There were four stations of guards taking off the chains simultaneously. Four were unchained, another four inmates were brought out. For over an hour the sound of chains being thrown into the fifty gallon barrels was prevalent. Finally, the last of the 120 men were free of the shackles they had been wearing for hours on end. What a relief!

We were then subjected to the long process of going through R&D. By the time we were assigned a bunk in the Arkansas Unit, it was around midnight. I was totally exhausted and so was everyone else.

The Arkansas Unit was draconian in comparison to anything I had seen yet. This was a huge building for prisoners who were in transit.

Inside this building were two four-story buildings that were attached by a set of steel steps weaving up to the top floor. There was one phone on each landing of steps, and there was a waiting line of about ten men continuously. There were ninety-six men to each floor and it was full year round.

The entire outside of the two buildings were surrounded by chain link fence. There are narrow walkways outside each cell on every floor and you had to use the steel steps to go up and down. Every cell had old steel-barred doors and was operated by electronic switches. Every night at 9:00 P.M. we were locked down for the night.

I asked around to find out how long I would have to be there and nobody seemed to know. All I got was maybe tomorrow and maybe a month from now. Great!

The Arkansas Unit was like a giant county jail in that we were locked down all day again. The days dragged by and the nights were terribly slow. The not knowing was the worst part. I decided to use this time again for reading the Bible. I found one lying on a bookshelf by the officer's station and began to read. These times that seemed so wasteful turned out to be a blessing when I trusted the Lord and let Him give me peace through His Word.

My desire hadn't changed for His Word, and I devoured page after page. For the first time in my life, I began to know the history of events of the Bible. I began to notice names and places I had read about before. This made it all the more exciting. I began to read the Old Testament now. It was much longer than the New Testament, but if I was going to know what God had to say, I had to read the whole book. God was working in my life even though I couldn't see Him. He was gently speaking to me as a father would speak to his son. He was showing me things that I didn't have the time or desire to see before. Now all I had was time.

CHAPTER 6

The 24-Hour Watch

Finally, after a week in El Reno, Oklahoma, Prison it was my turn to leave. At 5:00 A.M. I heard the guard standing outside my cell say, "Cox?" I said, "Yeah." I saw him look down to another guard and motion to him. My cell door opened electronically. It creaked as the door slowly made its way open. This door had undoubtedly opened hundreds of thousands of times over the fifty to sixty years that El Reno had been open. I dressed in seconds and as soon as I walked out to the fenced-in walkway, the door closed again.

After being processed, another 120 men were bused back to Oklahoma City to catch a ride on Conair. The inmate gossip was that Terre Haute, Indiana, was the first stop. Most of the time the inmates knew exactly what was going on.

Terre Haute, Indiana, was the closest federal drop-off point to East St. Louis, Illinois. Sure enough, the first stop was Terre Haute. I was taken off the plane and put in the custody of the Marshals again. This time, though, I was taken in the backseat of a car instead of a bus. It seemed you never traveled the same way twice when the Marshals picked you up.

All too soon I was back at the dreaded St. Clair County Jail, except this time I was housed in the federal block immediately. And I was put in AA-Block which is 100 percent federal prisoners. What a change. The only thing that bothered me was that Bob White was still in AB-Block right next door. How would I continue my private Bible studies?

I quickly found that at one end of the cell and at the top of the staircase there is a door that divided the two federal blocks. I could talk to Bob through this door. We couldn't see each other, but for now we could at least communicate, thank God. Our plan was for him to slide Bible studies under the door for me to complete and he would go over them. In the meantime, we started praying for him to be transferred over to my block.

I began to see my family and friends again. It was so wonderful to see them even for a few minutes each week. I lived for those times. Everyone continued to encourage me and that brought my spirits up. That was very important to me.

I got right back into church and Bible studies in the Chapel. The Chapel was really just a small courtroom by day and a church at night. It seated maybe twenty men. One great thing was that even though Bob and I were separated, we were able to attend church and Bible studies together. I continued to grow in the Lord and His Word even in that spiritual desert.

My new lawyer came to see me on a regular basis to prepare my defense. We seemed to be making some headway. At this point another bond hearing was out of the question. I wasn't going anywhere until the trial. So we went full speed ahead with our preparation.

One evening when I came back from church, everybody was buzzing about a fight in another block. It seems there were two guys who couldn't get along and they settled it with fists. That's if anything can ever be settled by fists. Even though one guy clearly won the fight, it's not over until it's over in jail. The guy who lost the fight waited until the other man was not paying attention and took a mop wringer from the mop bucket and smashed him in the face with it. The mop wringer ripped the man's face wide open and he was getting stitches in the infirmary. That was it. No more movement for that night.

There were now only three weeks until my trial date. Three weeks until my fate would be settled. I was getting very nervous and I began to feel uncertain about my defense. I just wasn't happy with the progress that my attorney had made. After all, my future was riding on my defense.

Then another surprise was dropped in our laps by the prosecution. I was notified to call my lawyer as soon as possible. When I got him on the phone, he told me the government had asked for a continuance. The judge had granted it. What did this mean?

It meant the judge had decided the prosecution had good reason to take more time for their case against me even though I had already been in custody for six months, over two times the seventy-day speedy trial rule which I had forfeited. The judge was going to set a new court date in the future that fit his busy schedule. It was horrible enough to have to go to trial, but it was just as horrible to have to wait even longer in that hellhole.

My lawyer and I talked about the situation. We decided that he would now ask the judge for another medical transfer back to Rochester Medical Prison until the judge set another trial date. He would also come to Rochester to visit and continue to prepare my case in my absence. The judge granted our motion and I began to set my mind toward travel back through the Prison System via Conair.

Only days before I was to be sent back to Rochester, I heard the doors open to my block. Everyone always looked to see who was coming or going because it was a really big deal. One new person in the cellblock could change your life in a place like that. The door slid open and in walked Bob White. Our prayers had been answered.

We began to study the Bible again every night and pray for our families and friends like we used to. You would be surprised how many "tough guys" would come by the cell and casually ask us to pray for them and their family. I don't care how tough you are, when you're alone in prison you might cry like a baby. Even tough guys need God. I know!

I remember one day when I was waiting for a visit. I never knew for sure who would be there, but I always knew someone would be, so I watched the clock for visiting time.

As I watched the clock and paced the floor outside my cell, I decided to go back to my cell and get something. I sat down on the bottom bunk just for a second and when I stood up to leave, I wasn't careful of the upper bunk and I felt a sharp pain in the top of my head.

I reached up and felt my head and blood was everywhere. I had ripped my head open on the corner of the upper steel bunk. I knew I was going to be called to a visit any minute so I pressed a cold, wet napkin into the cut. I held it tight and after about five minutes the bleeding stopped. I knew that if I told the officer about the incident, I would be sent directly to the infirmary and miss my visit. The cut could wait, but my visit couldn't!

I had a wonderful visit, and when I got back to my cell I waited a few minutes before I asked to see a doctor. The area that had been cut was matted with clots of blood so I ran water on it until the area was clean and bleeding freely again. I went to control and told them what had happened. They called the infirmary and then sent me with a guard to see the PA.

The PA examined the cut and told me he was going to have to stitch it up. He shaved the spot and gave me three stitches. Wow! That worked out perfect. I had a wonderful visit, and I also got the medical attention I needed.

Men were coming in and out of AA-Block. There was never any good news. It seemed like everyone was getting some serious sentences. One man got seventy-five years in a penitentiary. Others were facing serious time like I was. But I only heard of one man ever winning and his lawyer was Burton Shostack from St. Louis. Burton was a high-powered criminal lawyer.

My mother continued to visit and support me. She had offered to do as much legwork as was needed for my attorney, but he didn't seem to have any assignments for her. Still many of the visits were just really taking time to get to know each other again. It was a very important time in my life. I shared with her the things I had learned from the Bible. She was a willing student and became more and more aware of spiritual things. We prayed together every visit—something we had never done in all my years.

With the government you never know exactly when you will be moved even if you know you are going to be moved. For days I had expected to leave, but I didn't. Then the familiar, "Bunk and junk, Cox," rang through the block.

I had no idea how I would be transported. I did know from my last experience the only rule was there were no rules with the feds. This trip would be no exception.

I was loaded in a van with four other prisoners and we headed away from St. Clair. As usual someone asked where we were going and as usual they wouldn't tell us. Like always, we just had to wait. I had always been impatient, so this was worse than a beating for me.

I knew the area well because I had grown up there. As we approached the turnoff for Highway 70 East to Terre Haute, Indiana, the van driver just kept driving straight north. North? Where in the world were we going?

After about three hours we were all starving and had to go to the bathroom. The Marshals drove into a McDonald's. One Marshal took orders and the other one took us to an outside bathroom at the McDonald's. Keep in mind that there were five of us in full handcuffs, waist chains and leg irons.

One at a time we were allowed to go to the bathroom. I couldn't wait for my turn. I was ready to pop. Finally, I got in the bathroom. But the Marshal held the door open and stood so close I couldn't go. No matter how hard I tried I couldn't go. I was humiliated by his closeness. Finally, he said to either go or get out. I got out.

I lost my turn and had to return to the van. For just a moment I forgot about the bathroom because we had McDonald's. When you haven't had McDonald's for as long as me, everything was like a gourmet dinner. I had two cheeseburgers, fries and a chocolate shake. I was in ecstasy for a while, then it hit me again—I had to go bad!

Two more hours passed and I was about to turn blue. Finally, we pulled into the Metropolitan Correctional Center (MCC) in Chicago. It was a twenty-one story medium security prison one block south of the financial district on the corner of Van Buren and Clark. You could actually see Lake Michigan from the tenth floor up. MCC Chicago is also only one block from the federal court building in Chicago and daily the Marshals took prisoners wearing orange jumpsuits with chains down the sidewalk to court.

From the second I walked in MCC I knew I hated it. Even though it was a federal prison it was just like a giant county jail. I was locked down in a small area that was used for pretrial detainees. The floor was packed with men from the Chicago area waiting to go to trial. I couldn't believe it. Once again the feds could have taken me directly to the airfield at Terre Haute and flown me to Rochester that day, but nooooo! I was driven on a miserable van ride, in which my bladder almost burst, to a prison in Chicago to wait for the Conair to pick me up en route to Rochester. Once again, no one there knew how long I would be there. I just had to wait.

Let me explain how the flight pattern goes for the federal system for transporting a prisoner from East St. Louis, Illinois, to Rochester, Minnesota. All flights in the mid-central region originate and end in Oklahoma City, Oklahoma. The flight pattern encompasses a large circle and returns to Oklahoma City. So the original flight began in Oklahoma City, then stopped at Terre Haute, Indiana, then Milan, Michigan, then MCC, Chicago, Illinois, then Rochester, Minnesota, then Sioux Falls, South Dakota. Then the flight returns to Oklahoma City, Oklahoma, for the night.

My point is that the Marshals could have driven us to the airport in Terre Haute, Indiana, which is a two-and-a-half-hour drive, and I would have been in Rochester that day about eight hours later.

I spent a pathetically slow week at MCC Chicago and then I was back on Conair. From Chicago our first stop was Rochester. The Marshals had driven us all the way to Chicago, which is a six-hour drive from East. St. Louis, Illinois, and made us sit for a week to catch the Conair flight to Rochester when they could have gotten us there in the same day and saved thousands of dollars. You figure it out!

As sad as it seems, I was actually glad to be back in Rochester Prison. At least I had a mission there. There were prisoners who needed my help in 9-Building and I was excited to get back to work. As soon as I was assigned back to 10-Building I got in touch with the chaplain. He said he would be glad to have me back as a Hospice volunteer.

I was back in 9-Building within the first week and I had been reassigned to Walter. The inmate who had been assisting Walter was glad to be relieved. Walter wasn't the easiest man in the world to get along with, but I had missed the cantankerous old cuss. I needed to be needed and there I was needed.

I was medically unassigned so I wasn't obligated to work, but I've never been lazy so I started to look for a job. I wanted to work. The most logical place for me to work was in the Recreation Department. I had been a professional fitness trainer and gym owner for years before my arrest.

I soon found that I wasn't the only one looking for a job in Recreation. Everyone wanted to work in Recreation and there was a waiting list, but that didn't stop me. I went to the Recreation Office and asked to talk to the Boss. All the Recreation Staff just happened to be in the office the day I had decided to apply for a job. So I just started telling them about my prior experience with weight training and running fitness clubs. Little did I know that there is usually no comparison with what you know and who they hire in prison. After I finished my verbal resume, they just looked at me and said, "Sorry we are overstaffed as it is. We don't need anyone, and we don't hire pretrial inmates."

I left there feeling somewhat deflated, but others did tell me it was real hard to get a job in Recreation so I shrugged it off.

The next day I heard my name called to report to the Recreation Department. I went over and reported in. There was a Recreation staff member there who was present for my self-imposed interview the day before. He told me to sit down. He went on to tell me that although they were overstaffed and I was a pretrial inmate, some men would be leaving soon and he had been wanting to implement a new workout program. He felt I was just the man to get the program underway. He had talked to my Unit Manager and got me cleared to work for him. He explained what he needed and I started the next day. Now I was able to work full time and still do volunteer work for Hospice. I thanked God for opening those closed doors again.

Rochester, Minnesota, is a ten-hour drive from where I live. It's a long drive for my family, but I have to admit I didn't argue too much when they said they were coming to see me.

Visiting is so much different in prison. The visiting rooms are usually large enough to accommodate all visitors on a given day. I went to laundry and told them I had a visit coming and they gave me some new clothes to wear for the visit. I was instructed to keep these new clothes in good condition because I wouldn't get any more.

When the day came to visit, I was able to hug my family and sit with them at the same table all day. And the next day, on Sunday, we were able to attend church together. We held hands during the prayers and I could feel the love and care that my family had for me. It was a difficult time for me, but having family who cared made everything so much easier. Many of the men had no one.

Soon after my visit I was called to the Chapel. I went over and all the inmate volunteers were there for a special meeting. The chaplain told us that Mr. Thompson had been given two months to live. Mr. Thompson was an older man with no family. He had been in prison for years, and even though he wasn't my patient, I knew a lot about him from the meetings we had each week. Each volunteer talked about how their patient was doing and all the little things that went with each different personality. This was important because in the event someone had to leave without notice, others would know what kind of care and attention each inmate patient preferred.

The chaplain told us that we were going into a twenty-four-hour watch program. I had heard about it, but I had never been involved in it before. The chaplain had a blank schedule and we began to volunteer for four-hour blocks that would put someone with Mr. Thompson twenty-four hours a day until his time.

I volunteered for as many shifts a week as I felt I could handle. Normally, a volunteer worker would go into 9-Building at the evening meal and stay for about an hour and help out with things, then maybe go back and visit their patient for a while in the evening. Most of us were pretty dedicated and made it a point to visit our inmate patient each night if possible.

The first time I sat with Mr. Thompson he was very weak. I remembered seeing him in a wheelchair on the Yard just a few months before, being pushed by his volunteer. Mr. Thompson was a black man, but I didn't see black or white. I only saw a man whom God loved as much as He loved me. He was a man who needed a family, and we, the volunteers, were his only family now.

Mr. Thompson had tubes of oxygen up his nose and was bedridden. He was very quiet and he knew he was dying. I saw him get progressively worse day by day. Most of the time he didn't say anything, but he always smiled when he saw one of us come in. At first we helped him to the toilet, but as he got worse he had to use a bedpan. I usually just sat and read the Bible while I was there and occasionally said silent prayers for him.

Then one day one of the other volunteers asked me to trade shifts with him because he had some obligation that he had to fulfill at the same time he was scheduled to sit with Mr. Thompson. No problem for me so we traded shifts.

Mr. Thompson was now on a morphine drip to ease the severe pain from the torturous death of cancer. He was skin and bones. When I came into the room that evening he couldn't speak, but he motioned for me to leave the lights on in the room. I acknowledged that I understood and left them on as it got dark.

My shift with Mr. Thompson that night was 6:00 P.M. to 10:00 P.M. Around 8:00 I noticed his breathing became very irregular. It became slower and slower. As I read the Bible I looked up at him more frequently. Then as I was staring at him, I just knew he had passed from this life. I felt somewhat overwhelmed in that moment to be the last person that would ever see Mr. Thompson take a breath. I said a silent prayer for his soul and went to the nurses' station and told them I thought Mr. Thompson had expired.

They came running with stethoscopes and checked for a heartbeat. When they found none, they noted time of death for the coroner. Then they thanked me and told me to go back to my unit.

I knew it was the policy of the Bureau of Prisons to handcuff the deceased and put him in a body bag. Even when you're dead, you still don't leave prison without being cuffed. I wasn't allowed to witness this event so I wandered back to my unit.

I thought about the events that had taken place. This wasn't my scheduled shift. I traded shifts and Mr. Thompson died in my presence. This had to be God's plan that I would be there when he died. But why? Why me? Was the Lord preparing me for something that I wasn't aware of? Only time would tell.

Soon after Mr. Thompson died, I was notified through my case manager that a new court date had been set and that once again I would be leaving to go back to St. Clair County Jail. Once again I was apprehensive about leaving, but I had to get this trial over so I had to go.

I went to the chapel and poured my heart out to God. I knew now that He was with me always. I knew I would have to travel a road that very few people would ever travel and endure things that most people would never dream of, but I knew I wouldn't travel this path alone, for my Maker was with me.

CHAPTER 7

The 23rd Psalm

Once again I was on my way back to St. Clair from Rochester Prison. I had to go through El Reno, Oklahoma, only this time it was even worse than the first time.

When we got there we found out that El Reno was full (over capacity), but they were still bringing in another 120 men. By the time we had gone through the slow process of being admitted to El Reno through R&D, it was 1:30 A.M. We were absolutely exhausted.

It was mid November and for this time of year it was extremely cold. When we got to the Arkansas Unit we saw that there were cots set up all the way around the two center buildings that housed the inmates. The building was huge and it accommodated all 120 men. The biggest problem was that it was freezing cold against the brick walls where the cots were set up.

I had on all of my clothes—an Army jacket, shoes and socks, plus a wool blanket and I was still so cold I could barely sleep even in my exhausted state.

Thank God, the next morning they shipped out another 120 men so the following night we could be assigned to our cells. I sat through another grueling week at El Reno. There are planes that fly through Oklahoma City to pick up passengers from El Reno and fly to all parts of the country.

There is the east coast run, the west coast run, the southern run and the mid-central run. Most inmates knew there was only one flight a week going to the location they were headed. So if I knew that the mid-central run came through Oklahoma City on Tuesdays I would start holding my breath on Monday night.

Every morning the guards would come through at 5:00 A.M. calling out the names of the inmates who were leaving that morning. I guarantee, every inmate was praying to get out of El Reno on the day that he knew his flight would be coming through Oklahoma City.

I came in on a Tuesday and the next Monday I started praying extra hard, because I knew if I missed the Tuesday run I wouldn't have a chance to get out of there until the following Tuesday.

I was fortunate to get out after only one week. I had talked to other men who had been there for a month already. Your life is on hold there. You can't do anything or go anywhere. It seems like the days stand still.

When I got back to St. Clair, I was put in AA-Block again, the hold-over block for federal prisoners. My old friend Bob White was one of the first to greet me. We prayed and thanked the Lord for my safe passage through the system so far and began to redouble our efforts to study the Bible.

I was assigned to a cell by myself, at least for the time being. You never knew who was coming or going in St. Clair. One day you were sure you would be there for quite some time and then the next day you were gone. But for the time being, I had a bottom bunk and I was close to home. I was as happy as the circumstances would permit.

I sat in my cell and reflected the next day. I remembered back to when I went off on my lawyer for not getting a bond hearing within four days of my arrest. I remembered I couldn't believe I would have to be there for another three weeks waiting for my second bond hearing after I had lost the first one. It seemed like a lifetime since those things had taken place.

It was now December and I had already been in custody for nine months. I had never been able to secure a bond. I had never been to trial and I had already been in a Penitentiary, two medium security prisons, and two county jails. I thought back to when I was sure I couldn't even do three more weeks in St. Clair, and now I was still there nine months later. A lot had happened and there was surely more to come.

My court date was scheduled for January 1992. Again I was getting anxious, trying to feel good about my defense. Even though my lawyer had come to visit me in Rochester, I felt we had a better social visit than an attorney-client visit. It just didn't seem like we accomplished much against the prosecution's allegations.

Then, as time became shorter and my trial drew nearer, my lawyer seemed to be a little slack in his efforts to visit me. He would schedule a visit and then miss. That wasn't a good time to lose any time. I became increasingly concerned. I told my family and friends I was concerned with my lawyer's lack of effort on my behalf.

I was called out of my cell about two weeks before my trial. I wasn't sure who I was going to see, but I was hoping it was my lawyer. When I got in the attorney visit room, there was a man I had never seen before. The guard let me in and the man stood and introduced himself. "Hi, Danny. My name is Burton Shostack. Your family is concerned about you and frankly so am I. I have been retained to interview you to see if there might be anything I could do to help in your present situation."

Wow! The famous Burt Shostack from St. Louis, Missouri. He was a legend at St. Clair County Jail. He was the only lawyer to get anyone acquitted that we knew of and I was actually talking to him. I said, "Pleased to meet you, Sir. I could sure use some help."

We talked for quite sometime and I was very impressed at how professional Mr. Shostack was. He told me how he would conduct his defense if I were to decide I wanted him to represent me. I felt like an anvil was lifted from my shoulders. I felt like I had someone who cared what was going to happen to me. Someone who would put forth maximum effort on my behalf.

I wrote a letter to my present lawyer thanking him for his services up to that point and told him I would no longer require his services. So Shostack filed a notice in court that he would now be my legal counsel. Burt also contacted my previous lawyer and they made arrangements for him to pick up everything that he had compiled to that point.

My spirits soared. I could do this thing now. I had fire power. I was sure I had a good chance at beating this thing. I slept better at night and I was smiling all the time. I was going first class again. The Lord was full of surprises, and I thanked Him for opening another door that had been closed.

January was a deep freeze. One night in particular I was so cold that I couldn't even think. I was still alone in my cell and it was after the 9:00 P.M. lockdown. At 9:00 P.M. every man had to go to their cell for the night and each door was locked until breakfast in the morning.

It got colder and colder and there was no heat in my cell. The speaker in my cell was broken, so I had no way to contact the guard in control. I had on my two jumpsuits, two T-shirts, two pair of underwear, two pair of socks, and I was wrapped in two wool blankets. I was still freezing. It was that cold! I didn't know what to do.

I looked around and I saw my transcripts. My transcripts were all the papers I had received from my lawyer from prosecution. My whole defense rested on using these transcripts as a source of reference. There were some matches in the cell from the guy who was there before me. I got an idea. Desperate men have desperate ideas!

I had to build a fire, but where? I took a wax-covered box that had donuts in it and ripped it into a small square. I sat the wax square in the stainless steel toilet in my cell. Great! it floated! Now I began to tear up sheets of my transcripts into small pieces. I piled the small pieces on the wax square in the toilet. Then I lit the paper. A fire burst into flames.

I put my numb fingers over it and soaked up the heat. I practically hovered over the flame. I could feel the welcomed heat begin to penetrate the layers of clothing and blankets. When the fire got low I slowly dropped more pieces of my transcripts on the wax to keep the heat coming.

After awhile the wax square began to sink so I made another one. I was conservative after I got the cell warm enough to relax. I sat right by the toilet and thanked God for a way out of this intolerable situation. It was now unpleasant, but not impossible. After all, I had to make it through the night before I could make it to trial!

That was the only night that was so cold. The weather warmed up and so did my case. It was time for another curve. After all, it had been close to a month since anything strange had happened.

I got a message to call my new attorney, Burt Shostack. He told me he would be there that night and he had something important to tell me. Shostack is a stylish dresser, that went along perfectly with the fact that he was so successful. As usual, he was all business. He told me he had hired the best detective available to investigate the credibility of the two main witnesses against me. They were my unindicted co-conspirators. This meant that they were considered just as much involved in this case as I was, except they hadn't been charged because they were cooperating with prosecution.

Shostack also told me that this would take time and he wanted my approval to ask for a continuance of my trial. He wanted to ask the judge to postpone my trial for an indefinite period so he could put together the best defense possible. I had no choice so I agreed.

Then he said that since this would take some legwork and time, he would petition the courts to send me back to Rochester to evaluate the treatment I had received the last time I was there. From Mr. Shostack's countless meetings with men held in St. Clair County, he knew what a living hell it was to be there. He knew that I preferred the prison over St. Clair so he was one step ahead of me. I agreed to this also.

While I was waiting for the judge to rule on the motions, my mother found that Jack Stone had been transferred to Rochester Federal Medical Prison the week before. Jack had pled guilty and was sentenced to six-and-a-half years. I couldn't believe my ears. If the judge approved the motion, I would be seeing my old friend Jack in a short while. A few days later, I was notified that the judge had granted all the motions Shostack had filed, and in fact, I would be leaving soon for Rochester.

The trip to Rochester had been relatively uneventful, but my stay this time would be anything but uneventful.

I was taken to the officer's station in 10-Building. As he was preparing to assign me a room, I looked at the floor room assignment board that was hanging on the wall. I quickly found Stone's name. He was in a two-man cell by himself. What a miracle! I asked the officer if I could be assigned to Stone's cell and he said okay.

I gathered all my stuff and headed for the cell. When I got there, Jack wasn't around so I went about making up my bunk and putting away the personal hygiene products that were issued to me. Soon after I finished getting organized, in walked Jack.

He walked up to me and introduced himself. I was shocked that he didn't recognize me. I said, "It's me, Danny Cox." Then it was his turn to be shocked. We shook hands and hugged. It was great to be with my old friend. Really great.

He began to apologize, but that wasn't necessary. I knew that being in the county jail can take a tremendous toll on anyone. I hadn't seen the sun for months, so I was white as a ghost and hadn't shaved for several days. After we had a little small talk, we both laughed because he didn't recognize me.

On the other hand, Jack looked great. He had been there long enough to get some color and start lifting weights again. Neither of us was in any hurry to go anywhere that evening, so we just brought each other up to date on our situations.

Here is one thing I will never forget as long as I live. I began to talk about how my life had changed. I told Jack all about what happened to me that day I received the letter in the mail while I was in K-Block in St. Clair, how I had given my life to the Lord and was filled with peace. We talked for a long time about God. Then I asked Jack if he would also like to give his life to the Lord. He said he would. We prayed together (for the first time ever) and he asked Jesus to be Lord of his life. Praise be to God!

I found out that Jack was working in Education, which is in the same building as Recreation. I went back to my old boss and he hired me back that day. Jack and I started working out together. We had always worked out together before our arrest so this was great.

The chaplain also blessed me and gave me back my volunteer position in Hospice. Things were going great. Jack and I were assigned to the same cell; we practically worked together; and most of the time we were able to exercise together while we were at work.

About a month after I arrived in Rochester; Anna, Cathy, and Jacque, friends of mine from home told me that they were planning a trip to visit me. This was great news. I loved to have visits. I knew that going to Rochester was a lot of work and it was expensive. A few of my friends had decided to ride together and save money and share the ten-hour drive.

When my name was called to report to the visiting room, I was very excited. We had a really good time the first day, and I was in heaven because they were coming back the next day to visit on Sunday and go to church with me. This would be very special. I wanted my friends to spend time with me in church. I was proud that I had dedicated my life to the Lord.

My friends got there at 8:00 A.M. sharp and we visited all morning until the worst thing I could imagine happened. All of a sudden the visiting room was filled with guards. They were yelling, "All visiting is terminated. All visitors proceed to the opposite door to be escorted out of the prison." I was totally stunned and so were my visitors.

What in the world could be so wrong to cause all this commotion? My visit had just started and it was almost time to go to church. Then a guard screamed out, "Now people, let's go!" All inmates get over against the other wall and all visitors move toward the far door."

There was barely a second to say good-bye, so I grabbed quick hugs and I went to the opposite wall. Just that fast they were gone. What a heartbreaking feeling. I was sick inside. I felt like I had been run over by a truck and at that point I didn't care if I were to be run over by one.

We were strip-searched one by one, then sent back to our units by escort. When we got back into the compound we noticed the whole prison was already locked down except for the guys who had been on a visit.

When I got back to my cell, Jack told me the rumors that were flying around. He said supposedly three guys attacked a man at the weight pile on the Yard and cut his throat. They were trying to identify the three men who attacked him by any body marks.

Then we heard the sound of keys coming down the corridor. The guards yelled out, "Everybody out of your cell and stand against the wall. Take your shirts off and keep your mouths shut."

There were two Lieutenants and a Captain, plus the Unit Officer from 10-2. We stood there silent as we waited for them to get down to our cell. When they reached us, we were made to stretch out our hands and turn them over as they inspected us. Then we had to turn around and let them see our backs. God forbid if you had any kind of mark, even from sliding in softball or something, because if you did, you were going to the hole until they had time to do a complete investigation on you.

I couldn't believe it. What did I or anybody else in the visitors' room have to do with this? Why wouldn't they just go over the sign-in sheet at visiting and they would know who had visited for the entire morning that day. It would have been impossible to be involved if you had been in a visit all day.

My friends had driven all the way from St. Louis, Missouri, to see me and their visit was terminated early. The most important part— going to church with them for the first time—was gone.

I went from sick at heart to furious. This kind of thing can happen to you at anytime in prison. You can't control anything. In an instant, the most unlikely thing in the world can happen. You can be so happy and then you get the rug jerked out from under you like a cruel joke.

It might be months before they could visit again and maybe not at all. They were so kind to come all that way and they were treated so rudely. It was bad enough that I had to be treated like that, but not them. They didn't do anything wrong.

Later, I learned what had happened. There were two men who had bet on a card game. One guy lost and owed the other man fifty cents and was supposed to pay the winner the next week. When the next week came and the loser didn't pay the bet, the winner threatened that he had better pay up because he wouldn't let anyone disrespect him like that.

Two weeks after the bet went unpaid, there was trouble. When the loser was lifting weights on the weight pile in the Yard, the winner made his move. While the loser was bench-pressing, two friends of the winner came up and held the bar against the loser's neck. Then the man who had been cheated out of fifty cents took out a homemade razor and cut his throat. Then they ran.

In all high level prisons, there are guards somewhere on the yard. Somebody saw the man choking and bleeding to death and called the guards. Remember, Rochester is a Federal Medical Prison. They have a complete staff of doctors and nurses and a small, but well-equipped, hospital.

The guard radioed in an emergency situation and then hit "deuces" on his radio. When deuces come up on the radio, every staff member in the whole place has to go immediately to the location indicated on their body alarm. The place was crawling with staff and the emergency medical team was on the way with a stretcher and oxygen. The weight pile was about seventy-five yards from the hospital.

The medical team arrived and began to administer help in minutes. They took the injured man away and we never heard from him again. Later, somebody said that the guy who got his throat cut was named Thomas and they called him T for short.

They caught all the men who had attacked T and had them in the hole waiting to indict them on attempted murder. Later, we found out that the man who attacked T only had five months left to serve on a five-year sentence. He would have been home in five months, but now he was facing another fifteen years. All because he felt disrespected for a lousy fifty cents!

When I got back to Rochester this time, one of my friends there had been tending to my old patient, Walter. They were getting along well so they assigned me to another patient. Even though we all had an assigned patient, we always helped with anybody the nurses asked us to help.

Sometimes we would tend to three or four patients at a time. But that was perfectly okay with us because we were there to help and we wanted to help all we could.

Another emergency meeting was called. There was a man named Ted who had been given only a few weeks to live. We were going into a twenty-four-hour emergency watch. Our pledge was to never let a dying man be alone at any time in his last days.

Ted could have been released on a Compassionate Release, but his family didn't want him. Can you imagine being in prison and your family would rather you die there than to have you come home and be with them? This is what happened to Ted. No money, no family who wanted him, and no friends. No one to take him in for his last days. But we were there and we were honored to be his family in his last moments. I thank God for the compassion that He has instilled in my heart.

Ted began going in and out of consciousness soon after we started our twenty-four-hour watch. Ted was not my patient, but I learned that he had accepted the Lord and had changed his life a short time earlier. His last request was that at the time of his death, someone read the 23rd Psalm over him.

Ted got worse and worse until he was in a slight coma and on a continual morphine drip for pain. His body was all but dead, but his heart would not give up. He struggled day in and day out of a coma. We assisted the nurses in turning him to keep him from getting bedsores. There was not much else we could do but to be there with him and never let him be alone in his last days and hours. Another volunteer asked me to swap shifts. He had something to do so I took his morning shift and he took my midnight shift. I was there with Ted just quietly reading when I heard his breathing get slower and slower. It seemed like fifteen to twenty seconds between each breath. Another volunteer stopped by to see me and we were watching Ted. The pause became longer and longer and then he stopped breathing. I remembered Ted's last wish and quickly got my Bible and turned to Psalm 23. Like an old friend, I read the 23rd Psalm over him just as he requested. The other volunteer and I said a short prayer and then summoned staff. They entered and searched for signs of a heartbeat and then noted time of death. We were asked to leave while they prepared him for the coroner.

In a little while I walked back across the compound on the way to my unit. I glanced back at the hospital and I saw an old white hearse pulling into the back of the prison hospital. I knew that in moments Ted's handcuffed body would be put to rest. Ted had no money and no family who would claim him, so he would be buried in the unknown prisoners' graveyard there in Rochester. Ted's life was over from birth to death, and would sorrowfully end in the unknown prisoners' graveyard. No one to see him off and no tears to be shed. Just gone!

I walked back to my cell and reflected on the day's events. Once again, the Lord had put me there at the time of death. I had unknowingly traded into the only volunteer shift that would see the end of Ted's life. I felt empty, but in a way grateful to God that He had chosen me as the servant who would see Ted off to be with Him. There were ten volunteers and any one of us could have been there, but it was me whom the Lord had chosen.

No one knows our appointed day except the Lord. He alone knew the day, the hour, and the minute that Ted would leave this world to be with Him. And He chose me to be there. Again, I wondered why I was chosen.

I began to reflect on the sadness I felt for Ted because he had no family to grieve for him. What an awful tragedy. Then I wondered what could be worse than being in prison. A lone, bone-chilling thought came to mind as I searched for the answer. The only thing worse than being in prison was to die in prison!

CHAPTER 8

Dirty Laundry

Even though I worked a full-time job and was a volunteer for Hospice, I was involved in as many things as I could. When I was a member of Inmate Jaycees, I met Jim Bakker, the former PTL TV Evangelist. We were always doing something in Jaycees to make money. Then we would use the money to do something for the inmate population. For instance, we would pay for, prepare, and provide sandwiches and ice cream sundaes for the inmates during Super Bowl Sunday.

However, the Photo Club made more money than any other inmate organization. The reason was simple—Jim Bakker. Every Sunday the Photo Club took pictures in the Education Building. You received one picture for free and a second copy for $2.

Every Sunday Jim would donate his time to take pictures with anyone who wanted a picture with him. There was a line of inmates every Sunday waiting to get their picture with Jim. I got one shaking his hand. My family was amazed when I told them Bakker was there. I sent home a copy of my picture with him and my mother showed everyone. The picture is still on her wall.

I remember my mother and stepfather were coming to Rochester for a visit. I learned that Jim was going to have a visit that same weekend. My mother was hoping to get a picture with Bakker too.

When the day came to visit, my mother was really surprised when Tammy Faye walked in the visiting room. She asked me if I thought they would agree to take a picture with her, and I told her to ask and see.

In a moment, she came back smiling like crazy and said Tammy Faye was going to call her when they were ready. Soon they called her over and she stood between Jim and Tammy like she had known them all of her life. Jim and Tammy were very gracious and never turned anyone down. The picture turned out perfect. My mother always made the best of the circumstances.

Finally, I heard the dreaded news. The judge had set a date for my trial. I would be tried October 18, 1992 (eighteen months after I had been arrested). It was now the first of August and my lawyer wanted me back as soon as possible to work directly with him. Now it was a waiting game for them to come and get me again.

About a week later I was called to R&D. This was the normal way they did things except for one thing. I was called to R&D on the day the airlift flew. Usually, they call you down to turn in all your property the day before the airlift is scheduled. I was puzzled as to what was happening.

The next day I was called to R&D again. I went there and they cuffed me and prepared me to leave. But how was I going? The Conair plane that flew the mid-central route had flown the day before.

I was marched out of the prison and there was a bus with armed guards waiting for me. There were already about twenty-five men on the bus from other prisons. I sat down and they closed the steel screen door that separated the driver from the inmates. I looked back and there was another guard sitting behind another steel-screened wall holding a shotgun.

The bus door was closed and we were off. I asked some of the other prisoners to find out where we were going. The bus had just come from Sandstone and Duluth prisons in Minnesota. One man said we were on a route that would eventually swing through Terre Haute, Indiana. So that was it.

Riding a bus is not always easy. Hour after hour the trip gets harder and harder as you continually try to get in positions that make you feel comfortable while you are in chains After a while, there is no way possible to get comfortable.

Again, we were on the road all day in chains. Then the thought hit me. *Wait a minute, this is Thursday and the airlift only goes through Terre Haute, Indiana, on Tuesdays. What is going to happen to me when I get there? Where are they going to put me this time?* On the first night the bus stopped at the medium-high security prison in Oxford, Wisconsin. We were forced to spend the night there.

Just as the sun was going down on the second day the bus pulled into the parking lot of the Vigo County Jail in Terre Haute. Not again! Before long I was back in the same cell I was in there about six months earlier. This was the last place I wanted to be, but it was better than the Penitentiary, or was it?

I saw some of the same guys, but like always there were new faces. I went back into a four-man cell and I got an upper bunk. I noticed there was a lot of tension in the block.

After the second day there, two men got into an argument. One man threatened the other just before lockdown. In Vigo County the cells are in a straight line with one wall that is all steel bars and the doors close electronically. So when we were given the signal, every man had to step into his cell and the door closed automatically behind us. Then in a few minutes the guards came by to make sure everyone was in their cells and that everyone was accounted for.

With the one wall all bars, the men could talk back and forth as much as they wanted. You could hear others talking up and down the cell block.

The one man who had threatened the other one earlier, kept yelling and saying he was going to get him the minute the doors opened in the morning. He said he was getting his pencils ready and he was going to cut him up bad. He cussed and threatened for a long time and then it got quiet.

Then I could hear a different kind of noise and this one made me sick. I could hear what sounded like wrestling in a cell just down the way. I could hear heavy breathing and the kind of grunts that come with wrestling around. Then I heard a man say, "Okay, this isn't funny anymore. Stop. Stop. I said I don't like this. Please stop. Stop now!" And as the sounds of wrestling continued, the voice was silenced. No one said a word. I didn't know if it had happened often to that man or if this was the first time. All I know is the sound of someone being raped is sickening.

Then in the morning all hell broke loose. As soon as the sound of steel doors began to squeak open, the two men ran at each other. I saw them go by my cell swinging. One man had something wrapped around his hands but I couldn't tell what it was.

The cells were unloading into the walkway area to see the fight. Then the man that had been threatened hit the man that had threatened him all night one blow after another until he drove him the length of the cellblock. About this time the guards opened the door to serve breakfast. The man that had done all the talking started begging the guard to let him out because he said the other man was crazy and he had to get out of there.

The guard took him out and came back to serve breakfast like nothing happened. There was blood up and down the cellblock floor from the fight.

The winner was Buddy. A nice enough kid who had already done a few years of state time and was waiting to go back to prison. The man who had left had put sharpened pencils between each finger and knuckles and then wrapped his hands and wrists with torn up strips of t-shirt so he could have a weapon to cut Buddy's face to ribbons, but Buddy was more than this character had expected. Just because Buddy hadn't responded to his threats, he thought Buddy was scared and would be a pushover. In prison you never know whom you are dealing with until it is too late.

After spending another week at Vigo County Jail, it was time to go. When I was dressed, there were two Marshals there to pick me up. They had a car in the parking lot and I was going to ride back alone in the backseat. At least I knew this trip was only two-and-a-half hours to St. Clair County Jail. I could now do that standing on my head.

We crossed the Indiana-Illinois state line and traveled west toward St. Louis. The closer we got to home, the more exits I recognized. All of a sudden I heard the turn signal come on. I looked up and there was a sign for Vandalia, Illinois.

We turned off and drove toward Vandalia. We pulled into the Fayette County Jail. What in the world was I doing there? We were still thirty to forty minutes from St. Clair County. The Marshals took me in and turned me over to the Sheriff at Fayette County, then left. This place was a country bumpkin type place, but I had learned the hard way not to judge a book by its cover. I went through the usual process and was put in a holding cell by myself for the time being. This was kind of nice to be alone even for a few minutes.

Soon I was back in the old familiar orange jumpsuit that was the trademark of county jails. Then I was taken upstairs to a cell block. This place was very small. The block that I was going in held only ten men. This was about the smallest jail I had ever been in.

As soon as the men heard my voice talking to the jailer, they came out of their cells to see who was coming in. And who do you think was the first man to speak to me? My old Bible teacher Bob White. Praise God! Bob told me they had moved a few guys from St. Clair County to this place and he was one of them. This was wonderful. I didn't have to go back to the Gladiator School (at least for now), and my good friend and Bible teacher was transferred to Fayette County just before me. Once again I could see the Lord's hand moving in my life.

That jail was much farther for my family and friends to drive, but I was much safer there. I couldn't get as many visits there, but life was much simpler and for the time being I didn't complain.

Mr. Shostack came to see me soon after I was settled in Fayette County. He brought with him a very special man indeed. I was introduced to Dee Heil. Dee Heil is a private investigator. From what Shostack said, he was one of the best and the one he always used. Dee was a huge man, well over 300 pounds, and he had a deep, raspy, sandpaper type voice.

Dee had a long list of impressive credentials. He had been an Illinois Bureau of Investigation Detective for twenty years before he retired and went into private practice. He was a member of major case squad in Illinois. He had been around and he knew the ropes. I was to work closely with Dee in the preparation of my defense as far as my co-conspirators were concerned.

Dee and I got along well. He is a no-nonsense kind of a guy, and after all I had been through I really appreciated a man who was up front with me. I didn't always like what he had to say, but he was always straight with me and I appreciated it.

Dee and I were going to put together a defense to impeach the characters of the main witnesses against me. My mother had also asked to help with any legwork that she could handle. Mr. Shostack said she would be valuable in some areas to retrieve court documents and in other areas if she was willing. She was ready and willing.

Through the many jails and prisons where I had already served time, I had come to know many people who knew my unindicted co-conspirators. Even though I knew both of these men well, I learned things about them that I had no idea they had done. Both of these men had cooperated with the feds to put several people in jail.

It's interesting how large the penal system is in this country, yet how small it is in terms of being an information highway. One day a man could come in you had never seen before and he would know all about your case from somebody you knew in another jail. Everybody was in the same boat, so it was commonplace to help each other when possible.

It was now mid-August and there were only two months until my trial. Mr. Shostack said there would be no more continuances. The judge wanted my case tried on October 18, 1992. I had now been in custody for over sixteen months without bond.

From things I had learned while I was incarcerated, I gave Dee leads to follow. I knew a lot, but I needed someone else who was willing to cooperate with Dee and give him a signed affidavit verifying the things I already knew. To show the true character of these men, it had to come from some other source besides me and it had to be the truth. It had to come from people who were close to them.

The first co-conspirator we went after was Butch Conners. Butch had always been known as a thumper. A real tough guy. He had also been believed to be trustworthy in the underworld, but when the heat was on, he was one of the first ones to crumble.

Butch had been a murder suspect in his wife's death in 1981. They were driving on the Interstate near East St. Louis, Illinois, when he supposedly had car trouble. He said he pulled over and the next thing you know, two men showed up to rob them. They shot his wife in the head, shot him in the arm and drove away. He was a suspect in her slaying, but they could never prove he murdered her. Why was he a suspect beyond just being there at the scene? That's what my mother was going to track down while Dee would seek to get taped testimony from others about Butch.

Through a man I knew in St. Clair County, I found that Butch had busted a woman who was in another jail. When I found out that this woman, Lisa, had also given her life to the Lord I got her address and wrote her. I learned that Butch had been doing drug deals with her but he turned state's evidence against her.

She told me that he was suspected in the slaying of a Bond County construction business agent and that he had been called by the Grand Jury to testify. He was put in a county jail for obstruction of justice and then mysteriously released in a few days.

The wife of the man who had been slain was indicted and tried for his murder and convicted. This woman was a good friend of Butch's. She got thirty-five years and was in a state prison in Northern Illinois. Lisa gave me her name. She also told me I needed to have Dee talk to her seventeen-year-old son Tommy because he had something to tell us about Butch. She would personally arrange for this meeting. This was going to be our first big break.

Dee met with Tommy and this is what Tommy said in a sworn affidavit of his taped conversation: Tommy had started doing cocaine. His mother, Lisa, knew Butch very well. She knew he was a tough character, so she hired him to watch her son while she was out of town for a few days. Butch was to make sure Tommy didn't do any cocaine while she was gone.

Tommy said the first thing Butch did was to take him to a motel and handcuff him to a bed, then he left. Butch said he had business to take care of and he'd be back.

For days Butch dragged Tommy from motel to motel and cuffed him to the bed. Finally, Tommy said Butch came in and gave him some cocaine and some whiskey. He let Tommy get high and then told him that he'd sell cocaine to him for a real cheap price. He also said Butch slapped him around a lot the first few days. Just before he went back to his mother, Tommy said Butch gave him some cocaine to sell and told him he would pick up the money in a few days and not to tell his mother if he knew what was good for him. Again, Tommy was seventeen years old.

Dee contacted the woman who was in prison for murder. After several attempts, he persuaded her to talk to him about Butch. It was very difficult to get permission to take a tape recorder into a maximum security state prison, but he finally got permission from the Warden.

The woman's name was Betty. She said she and Butch had sold cocaine and marijuana together. She told an amazing story of what happened one time when she asked Butch to help her get back some drugs she had consigned to some guys who went to Florida and never came back with the drugs or the money.

Betty told Butch that she had been ripped off and if he'd help her she would pay him well. She had heard that a friend of the man that ripped her off was living in Belleville, Illinois. So they drove there to look for him. They knocked on his door and he answered in his t-shirt and shorts with no shoes. Butch put a gun to his head and asked where his buddy lived in Florida. He said he didn't know the address he only knew how to get there. That was his first mistake.

Butch grabbed the man and made him get in the backseat floor-board of his car at gunpoint. Butch wouldn't even let him get his shoes.

They were on their way to Florida, and this man was forced to lie in the floorboard in the backseat all the way there.

Betty said the man pleaded for Butch to stop so he could go to the bathroom, but he wouldn't stop. So the man on the floorboard finally urinated on himself.

When they got to Florida they found the house. Butch had the man's friend knock so the guy inside would open the door. As soon as the man opened the door, Butch busted inside and fired a round between his legs. That scared the man who lived there half to death.

Butch threatened to kill the man if he didn't come up with the money for the drugs. The guy said he didn't have all of it, but he gave Butch what he had. Then Butch went through his house and took everything of value he could get his hands on. He stole this man's possessions to cover the drug money owed to Betty because he was going to get a cut from whatever he recovered.

Just as quick as he left the house in Florida, Butch went to a store and bought the man from Belleville a pair of shorts and sandals and took him to the airport and told him to go home and keep his mouth shut or else.

Betty said Butch had threatened the man's life over a few thousand dollars in drug money. She believed he would have killed the man if he didn't have some way of paying back what he owed her.

Dee Heil was able to get the statements on tape from Tommy and Betty, and he had them put into transcripts from taped conversations. Then they were signed by each as sworn affidavits.

But that wasn't all. My mother had been searching around the area for proof that Butch was a violent man and not to be trusted. We needed documented proof and not just hearsay.

She went back and studied the newspapers at the time of Butch's wife's death. She found that Butch and his wife lived in a small town not too far from where we lived. She decided to make a visit to the local authorities there. The police there knew Butch well. They had had many run-ins with him over domestic disturbances. They had even served papers on him concerning his late wife.

My mother then went to the courthouse and purchased everything that was public information concerning Butch. What she found was amazing. Through the newspaper articles covering the death of Butch's wife in 1981, she discovered the police had been called out to their house numerous times because Butch had threatened to kill her. The newspapers also said that Butch's wife had finally filed for a restraining order because she feared for her life.

She was able to get copies of the actual police reports and remarks of the officers during the times they were called out by Butch's wife. She also obtained copies of the restraining order that ordered Butch to stay away from his wife. He could not go by the house or approach her without her prior consent or he would violate the restraining order. The list of complaints was very lengthy.

The police also volunteered other information. They said they knew Butch was dealing drugs in their area, but they had not been able to catch him. Others admitted they were very cautious around him because they feared him. He was known to carry a weapon at all times.

Now we had the documented proof Butch was a drug dealer, a suspect in two murders, had taken a man at gunpoint over four state lines against his will (kidnapping), had stolen private property from a man in Florida at gunpoint and threatened his life in front of two other people. Also, he had given liquor and sold drugs to a minor.

Everything was either in court documents or sworn testimonies from people close to Butch Conners. We also had enough newspaper articles about his violent nature to start a scrapbook. Now it was time to concentrate on Michael Mancini.

Michael was my other unindicted co-conspirator. These men were allegedly selling drugs with me, but there were no charges brought against them. They had both become government witnesses so the government elected not to hold them accountable for their actions no matter how severe they were.

I knew Michael better than Butch. I spent a lot of time with him. As a matter of fact, it was Michael and his girlfriend Terry who had originally talked me into smoking crack.

Mr. Shostack gave me a copy of everything the prosecution had given him concerning Michael. I learned that Michael had been under surveillance for quite some time. The feds had pictures of him in parking lots buying and selling large amounts of cocaine. They listed the name of the man he had been doing business with. They said Michael had been exchanging large amounts of cash for large amounts of cocaine. Within the police reports, there were thirty-six separate covert acts listed, but my name wasn't mentioned anywhere.

I found out that some years back, Michael had been seeing a certain young woman. Her father had been selling counterfeit money and

Michael decided to sell it with him. It wasn't long until the Treasury Department caught on and sent the feds to arrest him.

When the feds picked up Mancini for passing counterfeit money, they searched him and found cocaine. Now he was not only charged with counterfeiting, but also possession of an illegal substance.

Because he was a first-time offender, he was given a five-year probation. When I met Michael he was on probation. I knew that he had been in trouble, but that didn't bother me because he was a fun guy and I wasn't going to get involved with him in that way anyhow.

Then one night we went to a grand opening of a local nightclub. We were partying all evening and I lost sight of him several times. Michael drove to the grand opening that night so when it was time to go I had to find him. When I found him he was with two women and he said he would drive me home.

When we got to the parking lot a city police car pulled up and asked us to step back from the car. They said they had probable cause to search the car. They searched the car and found a bag of cocaine in the trunk. I had no idea.

Then they searched us and cuffed us and put us in the backseat of the squad car and took us to the station. They separated us and interrogated us. I had nothing to tell. I didn't know the cocaine was there and that was the truth. I didn't see Michael again that night. After about an hour, they just told me to go home. I called a cab and went home.

The next day, I found out that Michael had been granted another bond and was free until his trial date was set.

It was shortly after this that Michael and Terry talked me into smoking cocaine. I hated it the first time I tried it, but they kept begging me to give it another try. Finally, I did and the second time I was hooked instantly.

I reviewed Michael's situation. He had been arrested three years prior for counterfeit money and possession of an illegal substance. He had been convicted and was sentenced to a five-year probation.

He had since been charged with cocaine possession in the parking lot of the nightclub and was released on bond pending trial. Also, he was in violation of his first probation and was subject to spend the remainder of the two years of the probation in jail for violation.

Now, on top of these problems, he had charges stemming from thirty-six covert acts taking place in parking lots when he exchanged cash for drugs. All these charges were facing Michael and none of them involved me. My name was not involved in any of these cases. However, there were statements made by Michael that I had been involved with him in selling and possessing drugs. We were out to prove that this man would say anything about me or anybody else to get leniency for his many felony charges.

This last set of felony charges would make him a three-time felon. He was facing two years remaining in his first probationary period, five years for charges for possession of cocaine (found in his trunk), and now ten to thirty years for his current charges for sales of cocaine in parking lots that were verified by federal surveillance teams.

I read more and I was astounded. I discovered that all his charges had been dropped and instead he pleaded guilty to illegal use of a wire device (an illegal phone call). For this he was sentenced to one year in county jail. How could this be? Did the feds just forgive him for all that he had done if he would simply testify against me?

We also had sworn statements from people about Michael. Michael was a real party animal. He was known to always have a limousine for all occasions. He had a deal with a certain limo service and always had the same driver.

Dee Heil was able to get a sworn affidavit from Michael's limo driver that in all the times he had driven me and Michael that he had not seen me sell any cocaine to Michael. But he had seen Michael give me cocaine many times. We were able to get many sworn statements similar to these for my defense. Things were really coming together. My defense was shaping up and Mr. Shostack was very optimistic.

Mr. Shostack told me that in all his years as a criminal lawyer, he thought I had the best conspiracy defense he had represented, but still, even in this light, I only had a forty to sixty chance in favor of the prosecution.

CHAPTER 9

A 50/50 Shot

The days were slow in Fayette County Jail. There was no TV and no radio. Just the quiet cell block with most of the men sleeping their lives away. I walked up and down the narrow walkway outside our cells for hours trying to get exercise. There was no church and no gym.

As I walked I reflected about my daughter, Stephanie. Other than one visit from her in the St. Clair County Jail, I hadn't seen her or talked to her. Although it had been nearly a year-and-a-half since that visit, I still remembered it very clearly. She was eighteen at the time.

I had been in St. Clair about one month when Stephanie came to visit. I was very nervous and I know she was too. I was just sitting there in my orange jumpsuit with the phone in my hand behind the glass wall waiting for her. When she walked up in front of me, I motioned for her to pick up the phone on her side of the glass wall.

She did her best to force a smile, but I could tell she was very uncomfortable. We exchanged a few greetings and I asked her how she had been and she said, "Okay." This was one of the toughest conversations I have ever had. We only had a few minutes to visit so when her time was up I could see tears start to well in her eyes as she said good-bye. I didn't realize that when she said good-bye, I wouldn't see her again for close to a year-and-a-half.

But all of that was going to change that day because I was going to see my daughter. I was already getting nervous and there were still several hours before she would arrive. So much had happened to both of us in the past sixteen months.

Even though Stephanie didn't come back to see me after the one visit, her mother kept in contact with my mother. At least this way I was able to know how she was doing most of the time.

I had learned that my arrest had broken Stephanie's heart. She just couldn't face me again in those circumstances. The news of my arrest was on TV as well as in the newspapers. Different people reacted in different ways, but Stephanie had chosen to just avoid me. This was the only way she could cope with the situation.

Stephanie was living at home with her mother and stepdad when I was arrested. This was her third stepdad. I know that Stephanie had come to count on me in financial situations, but no matter how I tried to believe I was a great dad, I wasn't. Many times I made plans only to cancel at the last minute because I was high on drugs or planning another party. I was single, wild, and selfish.

I could see the pride in her face when she brought her friends to my racquetball club. And I once had a giant birthday party at my nightclub just for her and her friends on a day we were normally closed. I even had a DJ come in to play her favorite music and put on a laser light show for her and her friends.

She was proud that I was successful. She respected me and looked up to me. At least that is the way I wanted to see it. We had talked many times about what type of career she would pursue and had gone together to different schools and interviewed them concerning their curriculum. Stephanie graduated from high school just before I was arrested. I bought her a Ford Taurus for a graduation present. She was thrilled, but not as thrilled as I was to make her so happy.

As I walked back and forth on the concrete runway, I went over the things that had happened in her life in just the past few months. Because of what I had done I had lost my self-respect, my freedom, and my daughter. I was crushed. I loved my daughter and I wanted to see her so bad, but I felt so small and useless. So abandoned. So crippled by this whole humiliating experience.

A few hours after these thoughts flooded my mind, I heard the sound of the jailer's keys as he climbed the steps to my cell block. He called my name and I knew Stephanie was there to visit me. Sixteen months had passed since I had last seen her. She was almost twenty now and I wondered if she looked the same.

When we got to the bottom of the steps Stephanie was waiting for me. As soon as I saw her, I realized my baby was now a woman. She was smiling sincerely and the guard let me hug her. When we finished hugging I saw her wipe some tears away quickly. I was then put in a single cell right there by the jailer's desk. I pulled a chair up close to the bars and she pulled up to the outside of the bars.

The visit was still clumsy, but healing had begun for both of us. We were allowed to visit for a whole hour. The guard was pretty nice and I had been a model prisoner. He could hear everything we were saying and he knew this was a very important time for both of us.

We had a wonderful visit and after the guard gave us a five-minute warning, I reached through the steel bars and held her hands and we prayed together. That was the first time in my life I had prayed with my daughter and it felt very good. She gave me her new phone number, then she was gone.

There had been much healing that took place there that day. My door had always been open, but hers had been closed until that day. I thanked God that He had kept her safe.

I didn't get near as many visits in Fayette County Jail because it was much farther than St. Clair. However, my mother was my best visitor. She came up at least once a week. She was allowed attorney privileges there as well and we were able to visit in an attorney room as long as we wanted. My mother continually helped to prepare my case and always brought information from Mr. Shostack when he couldn't make it. She had done some fine legwork concerning my defense and had conferred with my legal detective, Mr. Heil, on many occasions. Everything was coming together very well.

As the last two weeks before my trial approached, I saw Mr. Shostack and Dee Heil more and more. Sometimes two or three times a week.

Dee Heil was quite a man. He had been a special investigator for a major case squad in our area before he retired. A veteran of twenty years of meritorious service, he was respected by most everyone. Not necessarily liked, but respected.

He had worked on a forensic team who had examined the crime scene and put together the evidence to convict many criminals. Now, he was in private practice using those same skills on my behalf. He had been in the courtroom many times and testified for prosecution. He was considered a specialist in his field. He had also been present when my attorney, Burt Shostack, defended some of his clients.

One day, shortly before my trial date, he told me he had seen both my prosecutor and my attorney in courtroom situations. He said in his professional opinion, he would give Mr. Shostack a sixty-forty edge over my prosecutor. He said Mr. Shostack was an expert criminal lawyer and the prosecution knew this.

Now, I had two different opinions. Mr. Shostack felt it was a sixty-forty situation in favor of the prosecution, and Mr. Heil felt it was a sixty-forty situation in my favor. If I were to add these two together, I had a fifty/fifty chance of walking out of the courtroom a free man as soon as the trial was over. The trial was going to begin in a week and in about three weeks after that I would know the answer.

During the last week, Mr. Shostack brought even more of his staff with him to counsel me. He explained in more detail what would transpire and began to prepare me for the actual courtroom proceedings.

We were going to attack the credibility of the prosecution's star witnesses, but I wouldn't be able to testify on my behalf. He said that would be too dangerous.

We were going to bring to light what scumbags these two men were. We would introduce into evidence all the many documents and affidavits we had. Our witnesses were ready to tell the stories firsthand of the gross atrocities that Butch Conners had perpetrated on them, how he had sold drugs to them and was a drug dealer who was always armed and dangerous. He was a kidnapper and a murder suspect. And how Michael Mancini was a third-time felon, a loser who would do or say anything to keep from getting a life sentence. The only thing powerful the prosecution had for evidence from Michael was his word and that was about to be destroyed.

I had a powerful case and I knew it. But why was I still feeling depressed inside? I was about to have my day. I could get even with those guys for all the pain and agony I had been through for the past eighteen months. This was going to be some sweet revenge, so why was there a nagging feeling inside my heart? Why did I feel like something was wrong?

My trial was to begin on Monday, but for some reason I began to soul-search in a deeper way than I had ever searched the Friday before. I began to look over the whole picture in my mind and heart. This was going to be a major event. There was going to be a battle of words. Prosecution was going to make a case that I had possessed and sold cocaine. We were, in turn, going to build a case by tearing down their case by undermining the character of their star witnesses.

We were going to bring out every dirty little secret that we had. We were going to show the jury, beyond a shadow of a doubt, just how pathetic these men were.

But what about me? Where did I fit in? What was my role in this whole thing? Why was I even having to defend myself in the first place?

For the past eighteen months straight I had studied the Bible. I was a new man inside. I had changed and I was still changing daily. The Lord had begun a work in my life and I wasn't a finished project by any stretch of the imagination, but I was certainly under construction. Late into the night on Friday I wrestled with my own conscience, my own soul. I couldn't find rest. I was plagued with many thoughts that I didn't want to have.

Yes, we were prepared to bare the souls of these men for the whole world to see, but did that change the facts any? Did this in any way make me not guilty?

I thought back over the original charges the DEA had shown me at Hardees Restaurant. How, after I wouldn't agree to cooperate with them against others, they came up with new charges to add to the original allegations against me. I remember my blood ran cold as ice as I read what was said about me. On two separate occasions I had unknowingly met with Butch Conners when he was wearing a wiring device. The taped conversations had been turned into transcripts and were now in the possession of the prosecution as well as the defense.

Not only had I met with Butch, but there was an entire surveillance team of law enforcement officers surrounding the location where we had met. Not only did they have audio tapes that they were soon going to play for the whole world to hear, but they had the confirmation on half a dozen law enforcement officers to this fact.

They had searched Butch before he met with me to make sure he didn't have any drugs on him. Then they searched him immediately after he met with me and found four ounces of cocaine on two separate occasions. Regardless of what Butch had done, I had sold him eight ounces of cocaine.

Then there was Michael Mancini. Although there was no hard evidence that I had ever sold him any illegal drugs, he was going to testify that I had sold him a large quantity over the past two years prior to my arrest.

And then there was the fact that I couldn't testify on my own behalf. My attorney was afraid I would incriminate myself. How could I do this if I was innocent?

The moment of truth had finally come. Was I innocent or guilty? Regardless of whether my unindicted co-conspirators had broken the law over and over, the point being—was I guilty? Could I go into the courtroom and play a game of who was best at making the jury believe that the other was the worst to be acquitted?

Sure, Michael was the guy who talked me into smoking cocaine, but I had a choice. I was a grown man and I made a choice on my own free will to smoke cocaine. Would it make me a better man if I put his dirty laundry on display for the whole world to see? Yes, I had been desperately hooked on cocaine at the time I sold drugs, but I still broke the law on my own free will.

Would it make me a better man if I were to bring out the violent acts of Butch Conners and make it known to the jury that he was a suspect in his wife's brutal slaying a few years back?

Then, on the other side of the coin, I thought about my charges. I was charged with conspiracy to sell drugs. *Webster's Dictionary* defines "conspiracy" as an agreement among two or more people to break the law.[2]

Anytime you sell anything there is someone you buy from and someone you sell to. And my situation was no different. What about these other people? These are the same people the feds told me that the government wanted me to testify against. As a matter of fact the DEA

---

[2] *Webster's Ninth New Collegiate Dictionary* (Merriam-Webster, Inc., 1990), 281.

had told me if I cooperated with them against these people my charges would just disappear. I had already gone through eighteen months of hell and I can tell you that their offer was beginning to look very good by this time.

I was facing a minimum of ten years in prison as a first-time offender. Why did I have to do all the time? Why shouldn't four or five of us do two years apiece? Wouldn't that make more sense?

I wanted to go home in the worst way, but I also had a new life to live—a new life in Christ. In 2 Corinthians 5:17 Paul explains this new life by saying, "Therefore, if anyone is in Christ, he is a new creation; old things have passed away; behold, all things have become new." My *New King James Study Bible* goes on to say that for everyone who has ever wanted the chance to start all over again in life, Jesus Christ gives them that opportunity.[3] No matter what you have done in the past or who you may have been, when you accept Jesus Christ, your past is totally forgiven and you become a brand-new person with a totally new identity in Him.

I had been forgiven by the Lord even if there were others who couldn't accept me. Would I now step back into the shoes of the man who was dead in sin or would I walk in the shoes of the new creation that Christ had made me? Would I do the right thing? Something I had not done well for the past thirty years?

I prayed with all my soul that night and in the morning I had reached a decision. I called my lawyer and asked him to meet me as soon as possible—it was an emergency!

---

[3]   *Spirit Filled Life Bible for Students*, NKJV, Ex. Ed., Jack W. Hayford (Thomas Nelson Publishers, 1995).

When Shostack got to Fayette County Jail, he was with Dee Heil. I sat down and told them I had decided to plead guilty. They were both shocked. I told them I had thought about it long and hard and I couldn't go on deceiving everyone, including them.

Shostack said he would call the prosecutor immediately and tell him I was going to change my plea. My only request was that I wanted to plead guilty straight up, no deals and no bargains.

What I had done I had to pay for. Regardless of the involvement of all the others in my conspiracy, I wouldn't cooperate with the government against others. I would assume my own responsibilities and that was all. That was the only way I could plead guilty. I had already served eighteen months for not cooperating and I wasn't going to change that part now. The minimum sentence I faced was ten years, so I asked for the minimum in exchange for my guilty plea.

Many people were shocked on my first day of trial as they heard me change my plea to guilty. I heard a low exchange of comments run through the courtroom just after the announcement.

Now everyone knew for sure. No more games and no more deceiving my family and friends. The ugly truth had finally come out, but I was also now free from the prison that had held such a tight grip on my soul for so many years.

On one hand I had been a respected businessman and on the other hand I was a cocaine addict and a drug dealer. I had led a double identity for so many years. For thirty years I had been "High on a Lie" and now I was free from the lies, but not free from the severe punishment that I had decided to face alone. God had forgiven my sins, but for my actions

I would have to suffer grave consequences. Remember this, God will forgive you, but the government will not!

So, on October 18, 1992, I admitted I was guilty as charged in front of my family, and worst of all, the news media. Only a small group of people were there to witness my admission of guilt, but by the following day the entire area read about it in the newspapers.

As far as Butch and Michael were concerned, they're still accountable for their actions too. It was apparent that the law wasn't going to hold them responsible for their atrocities because they were willing to testify against me and everyone else they could, but they still have to answer to God. We all do.

God knows everything we do, even those things done in secret. These men knew the horrible things they had done. And just because the feds had decided not to prosecute them in exchange for their testimony against others, it didn't make them any less guilty than me. And besides Butch and Michael, there are many other people involved in my conspiracy. They have not been found out, because I decided to protect them, but they are just as guilty as I am. These are people I bought drugs from and people I sold drugs to. As far as I was concerned, I did what was right and left the rest up to the Lord. All these people will have to stand before Him soon enough to give an accounting for their actions.

Revelation 20:11-12,15 says, "Then I saw a great white throne and Him who sat on it, from whose face the earth and the heaven fled away. And there was found no place for them. And I saw the dead, small and great, standing before God, and books were opened. And another book was opened, which is the Book of Life. And the dead were judged according to their works, by the things which were written in the books… And anyone not found written in the Book of Life was cast into the lake of fire."

CHAPTER 10

My Day in Court

The judge noted the change in plea and set a date for sentencing on January 8, 1993. I would now have to wait another three months in the county jail just to be sentenced and then officially be designated to my first prison.

The three months before my sentencing date passed very slowly, but finally January 8th arrived. I remember the bailiff telling everyone to rise as the Honorable Judge William Stheil entered the courtroom from his private chambers.

This time I wasn't wearing my old dirty clothes. I was wearing a freshly starched white shirt, paisley necktie, black slacks, and a jacket suitable for the occasion. I had also been blessed with a professional haircut just days before—something that no prisoner is accustomed to. My longtime friend and professional hairstylist Perry Hendrickson had come to see me in the Fayette County Jail. The Sheriff granted permission for him to cut my hair while he was there to visit me.

I glanced around the courtroom. The seating gallery was full. I saw family, friends, and a host of other professionals such as my investigator Dee Heil and news reporters. I knew that I wanted to get this over with and get on with my life. As unpleasant as it was going to be, it still had to be done.

The judge went over the charges that had been brought against me and asked me if I understood them. He then went over all the sentencing guidelines and mandatory minimums that applied to the charges and asked me if I understood them. He then asked me if my guilty plea was still in effect. Then he asked me if I understood the sentence that could be imposed on me according to the charges brought against me.

After I acknowledged that I understood each issue, the judge asked if I had anything to say to the court before he read my sentence. I said, "Yes, I do, Your Honor." I got up and every eye in the room was on me. The silence was deafening as I made my way to the bench directly in front of the judge.

These are the exact words that I have taken from the transcript that day on January 8, 1993:

> **The Court:** Mr. Cox, when you entered your plea, I told you that today you would be given time to tell me anything that you think I ought to consider before imposing sentence. I want to give you that opportunity now.
>
> **Mr. Cox:** Thank you, Sir. Your Honor, I have been a Federal Prisoner for the past twenty-two months. During this time the Bureau of Prisons has comprised a central file on me, a track record, if you will. In this central file the Bureau of Prisons has information in categories, such as work reports, education, volunteer programs, and so on. I believe that my central file will reflect a positive attitude as well as a positive change of heart. I'm truly sorry for what I've done. I ask forgiveness from God, from my family and my friends. I apologize to the court. I ask the court to have mercy. Thank you, Sir.

The Court: Mr. Shostack?

Mr. Shostack: As a matter of law, it is rather cut and dried. As a personal matter I'm bothered by the fact that among the many tragedies involved in this matter, it is that Danny Cox is a man of substance, and he had gotten himself in this position. However, I think that he has expressed himself well to you. I have spent enough time with him to know, and can tell you as an officer of the Court, that he means what he says.

He pleaded to the case. It was a straight up deal. The only deal really we had with the government is they would recommend a cap of ten years by virtue of the amount, and would not object his being sent to a camp, if that can be done. I have no reason to believe that the Government will do otherwise. The guidelines are the guidelines. Unfortunately, they have taken from you a great deal of discretion, but he must be sentenced according to what Congress says, and so what I say at this point beyond that would have no meaning or effect, and can't have, so consequently, we're ready to be sentenced.

The Court: All right, thank you. Mr. Garrison (prosecutor).

Mr. Garrison: Your Honor, I have nothing to add. Thank you, Sir.

The Court: Mr. Cox, this case had been before the Court for quite a long time.

Mr. Cox: Yes, Sir.

The Court: As you are more aware than I, part of it, as you know, had been due to your need for medical care.

Mr. Cox: Yes, Sir.

The Court: The Court understands that and my comment was not one of criticism. I am aware of the situation. I am aware also from other sources of what you have told me this afternoon about your conduct since you have been detained, the manner in which you have approached your situation. I believe you when you tell me that you are remorseful. I think you have demonstrated some of the remorse, so it gives some credibility to your statement.

In viewing your presentence report, other than those items we have mentioned a little earlier in this hearing, there had been no—there are no entries of any prior criminal conduct, so I take that into consideration as do the guidelines.

Mr. Cox: Yes, Sir.

The Court: As Mr. Shostack had indicated, you are aware that the Court is limited in its discretion in a case such as this, that not only are the guidelines applicable, but it is also a mandatory minimum sentence which has been established by Congress. The purpose of that, of course, is because Congress, reflecting the will of the people of this country, is cognizant of a great harm that is done to many people through the procedures and practices that you engaged in, which is the trafficking of narcotic substances, and that harm has now come full circle. It has harmed you, your friends and family, those whom you love. More importantly, it has harmed society in general, the people who consumed that product that you participated in dealing in. So that because of that great danger, the Congress had established very stringent penalties.

I am going to accept the Government's recommendations, which having made the ruling I did on the applicable guidelines, any discretion I might have had of one level discretion has been removed, and I will impose the penalty required by statute; believing though, that it is adequate to punish you for the crime that has been committed, as well as being adequate to serve as a deterrent to others.

I sometimes question that conclusion, seeing numbers of cases that go through this Court and all of the Courts, people engaging in that kind of enterprise. Apparently they don't realize the fact of heavy penalties or the fact of the terrible things that they are doing to their fellow man. I will now state the sentence I intend to impose, after which counsel will be given the opportunity to state any reasons they may have as to why it should not be so imposed.

Pursuant to the sentencing Reform Act of 1984, it is the judgment of this Court that the defendant, Danny Ray Cox, is hereby committed to the custody of the Bureau of Prisons for a term of 120 months.

When the judge said, "120 months" there was a hush over the courtroom. Then I could hear murmuring throughout the gallery. And even though I already knew I was going to get ten years, there was still a lump in my throat as the judge made it official. I tried not to think about it or show any negative emotion so I wouldn't hurt my family more than I already had. I was able to hold at least a small smile as the judge finished the hearing.

But possibly the hardest part was still to come when I had to turn and face the entire gallery on the way out.

I saw stunned faces amid teary eyes everywhere I looked. My mother and sisters were crying as I passed by with the Marshals escorting me downstairs to a holding cell. I did all I could to let them know everything was going to be all right with the cheeriest smile that I could muster. But inside I knew that the path I alone had to walk would take me away from my loved ones for years to come.

Soon after this, I learned that one of my close friends had said this about that day in court. He said if he hadn't known for sure, he wouldn't have been able to tell whether I was the lawyer or Shostack was the lawyer. Standing side by side in jackets and ties he said we both looked equal to the part.

We may have looked equal that day, but Mr. Shostack was going home to his family that day and I was leaving in chains to spend another eight years in Federal Prison.

CHAPTER 11

God Works in Mysterious Ways!

As I sat on the Conair plane on my way to a medium-security prison in Milan, Michigan, I thought about my only request at sentencing, besides a minimum ten-year sentence, which was to be designated to a prison camp. Milan, Michigan, Federal Prison was obviously no camp! Then I began to recount the events that had taken place over the past twenty-two months.

I had been held without bond (denied three times) for eighteen months prior to trial. I had already served time in one penitentiary, four medium-security prisons, and six county and city jails.

Now, just a few days over twenty-two months, I was going to my first officially designated federal prison. I had spent 637 days in jail and I was just now officially in prison. I recalled once again how I had blown up at my lawyer because it was going to be five days after my arrest before he could get me out through a bond hearing. I think a smile even came to my face. I guess that was better than crying.

As far as I was concerned Milan, Michigan, was a nightmare. There were anywhere from 1,400 to 1,600 men there at any given time. It was somewhat like a small city behind razor wire fences and manned gun towers.

The place was decrepit where I was housed and I was guessing the buildings were seventy-five years old or older. I got a job in the

Institution Warehouse unloading trucks at the rear dock. They had welders working twenty-four hours a day in Unicor, but I had to get on a waiting list if I wanted to work there. Those men could make up to $1 or more an hour. That was big wages considering almost everyone else made 12 cents an hour, including me.

The place was a zoo. There were fights, stabbings, gangs, and just a general uneasy attitude that kept me constantly watching my back. I wasn't looking for trouble and I didn't want trouble to find me.

Although Milan was the kind of a place you didn't trust very many people, there were some of the strongest Christian men there I have ever met. A few days after I arrived I went to my first Bible study. I met some good Christian brothers and began to meet with them regularly, twice a week, for about two-and-a-half hours.

They had just started a deep study on Revelation, the last chapter in the Bible. I had always kind of shied away from this chapter because it scared me. I guess we're all afraid of the things we don't understand, and I was no exception. I decided that it was time to stop avoiding Revelation and to seriously see what God had to say about the end times.

The inmate Bible teacher was truly called by God to teach. He had a fifty-year sentence, and you would have never guessed he was going to spend the rest of his life behind bars. He was a caring and knowledgeable teacher never showing anything but peace through the Lord.

I got to know the men who were regulars at the Bible studies pretty quickly and I saw them everywhere. They were always asking me what they could do for me. They said they all stuck together as Christian brothers and when one was in need they were all in need.

One thing for sure is there is a lot of talk about God in prison. Good and bad. Before I came to prison I don't remember anybody bringing up the subject about God much. The only time I heard His name was when someone used His name in vain, and that included me. This was a common occurrence with the group I hung around with. Not only did I not hear about God, but I had isolated myself from all religious people.

In prison you're immediately thrown into a mix of Catholics, Muslims, Moor's Science, Buddhists, New Age, Methodists, Jews, Baptists, Pentecostals, Lutherans, Jehovah Witnesses, as well as atheists and many more. There are many opinions on what is right and what is wrong, therefore many discussions are sparked.

All the Christian brothers were great. It was incredible that even in a spiritual desert, there was an oasis of God's people who carried their crosses for Him daily. I was so at home with these men. I hated Milan, but I loved the Bible studies and the closeness that I felt to God there.

I spent many nights studying the Word of God, but finally I was called down to my Case Manager's office and told I was being sent to a prison camp that was much closer to home. Over time my security level had dropped and I was now camp eligible. They said they were transferring me to the Federal Prison Camp in Terre Haute, Indiana. Terre Haute is just 160 miles from home and only a two-and-a-half hour drive. I couldn't wait to get closer to home. In all my time at Milan, I didn't get a single visit.

Within days, I was on a plane again and I was taken to Chicago, Illinois, to stay at the MCC Federal Prison until I was picked up by bus to go to Indiana. I was there a week when the bus arrived from picking up and dropping off prisoners from northern prisons. This was going to be my first camp and I was really excited. As I walked towards the bus I could tell that it was still about half full of prisoners. I made my way up the bus steps and who do you think was the first person I saw? Jack Stone! I couldn't believe my eyes and neither could he. Jack was on his way to the same camp from Sandstone Prison in Minnesota. There was a seat open next to him and I sat down and started catching up on all the things that had happened to him since the last time I had seen him.

It was a long ride and after awhile we both settled in for the trip and just appreciated the fact that two old friends were finally united and we were going to the same camp. Serving time in prison isn't pleasant, but at least I had my best friend to do it with now. I thanked God for yet another special blessing in my life.

As we sat there enjoying the scenery, I began to think about my new home at the camp and what God had in store for me there. My heart began to dream sweet dreams.

CHAPTER 12

Head Over Heels

I was amazed when I got to the prison camp. There were no fences and no guard towers. It had just four small housing units that held about 350 men, nothing like what I was used to. The atmosphere was light and nonviolent. I asked someone why the camp was so low-key. I was told you were supposed to be on your honor in a camp. No one wanted to fight because if you did you might be transferred to a higher level prison. That made sense.

Jack and I were not only put in the same room, but we were "bunkies." He got the lower bunk and I got the upper bunk. We had both been through so much already and now we were finally fairly close to home, and even though we were still in prison, it was great to have a lifelong friend to do my time with.

We also ran into another friend of ours, Terry Metcalf, from our hometown area. Terry had already been there for three years. He was "#1" on the camp construction crew, and he got Jack and me a job in construction with him.

One really bad thing about Terre Haute Camp was that it didn't have air-conditioned housing units. That first summer that I was there was one of the hottest summers recorded in Terre Haute history. It soared to over 100° over thirty different times.

The buildings were almost all steel and brick so when it was so hot outside, it was like an inferno inside. Inmates were taking showers all through the night to cool down enough to sleep. We worked outside all day in construction. Then when we went back to our housing units, it was still about 90° inside. That summer I lost close to ten pounds, but believe me, I was still not complaining.

Soon after I got there, I began to submit names to my counselor so I could get friends and family approved to visit. My mother and my stepfather George came immediately to see me, then others came. It was great to visit there and the visiting rooms were air- conditioned so that made it even nicer.

The weather turned really nice in the fall and I began to walk the outdoor track quite a bit with Jack and Terry. We all knew many of the same people and we had great times just walking and talking together. But there were also times when I liked to walk alone.

I had been single all my life, but there was something stirring in my heart that hadn't been there before. For the first time in my prison life, I began to think about a wife and when I walked alone, thoughts about a wife kept dominating my thoughts. I knew other men who had been married in prison, so I began to wonder if the Lord would actually bring me a wife in prison too.

Soon, I began to walk and pray for a wife. Have you ever prayed to God for a miracle and then told Him how to do it? Well, that's exactly what I did. I started to dream about what would be a perfect wife for me. Then I began to tell the Lord all the qualities that I thought she should possess (including a great figure).

After several weeks of praying this way, it came to me in my spirit one day that if I really trusted God and believed He was capable of bringing me a wife in prison, that I must trust Him in everything.

So, I changed my prayer from that day on and I asked the Lord to bring me a mate of His choice. One that would be perfect for me. I searched the Scriptures and read in Genesis 2:18 that the Lord would make a mate suitable for me—one who would be compatible to me intellectually, physically, and morally. Since I was already forty-five at the time I knew God had already made the perfect mate for me. Now all He had to do was to bring her to me because I couldn't go to her.

By this time it was late September. I had put several people on my visiting list, but I still had room for more. I did have several single attractive females on my visiting list, but no bells yet.

Then one day, I was talking to my brother on the phone. He said he had talked to a girl we both knew named Sandy. I asked him how she was doing and he said she looked great and seemed happy. I hadn't talked to her for a long time. I asked him to ask her if I could call her. So he said he would ask her and let me know.

My brother and Sandy had been close friends for years. As a matter of fact, just after the feds contacted me at my Tan Salon, but before I was arrested, my brother brought Sandy to my condo when he came to visit me.

As I lay on my bunk, my mind started to drift back to that time a few months before I was arrested. Then the time he brought Sandy to my condo with him. We all had a great time visiting and when she was leaving, I asked her for her number and I called her later.

We went out together a few times and almost instantly I felt like I had known her for years. We began to see each other regularly. I told her I was in serious trouble. I told her I thought I was going to be arrested by the feds at any time. She never wavered or backed off no matter how depressing the news.

To the contrary, she was very supportive and encouraged me to be strong. That was a time in my life that I was going through a nightmare every day. I knew that the feds had told me that if I didn't cooperate they were going to indict me, but they didn't tell me when. So every day I was looking over my shoulder and every night I felt like they might kick in my door at any minute.

Sandy was a good listener. I knew she had problems of her own, but she took the time to listen and console me at a time when I needed to be understood. This was only one of the many fine qualities that she possessed.

During my first week in St. Clair County Jail, I gave my life to the Lord. I couldn't wait to tell Sandy. I called her and told her the whole story just as it happened. I remember we both had goose bumps as I told the story. Then we cried together.

She told me that she too had accepted the Lord a few years earlier, and she remembered the incredible feeling too. We began to talk about the Lord all the time.

Sandy had come to see me as often as she could when I was in St. Clair. She always looked beautiful. Those were difficult times for both of us. We got along so well, but we could never be together. It was frustrating for us both and I was facing at least ten years in federal prison, not to mention that my court date was being postponed continuously.

Now my thoughts drifted back to the present. Back to Terre Haute Prison Camp and the conversation I had just had with my brother, in which he had told me he had recently seen Sandy. When he told me he had talked to her, I wanted to talk to her too. I missed her.

The next time I talked to my brother, he told me he had talked to Sandy and she had a steady boyfriend. She had given me permission to call, but I had to call her at work, not at home. I understood and agreed.

Our first conversation was very clumsy to say the least, but it was nice to talk to her again. I didn't mention her boyfriend.

After a few calls I couldn't contain myself, so I asked her if she might ever want to visit since I was only 160 miles away. She hesitated for a moment and then said she would think it over. In the meantime, I could send her a visiting request form, so I did.

By this time, my visiting list was full except for one spot. I sent her the form and soon after my counselor informed me that she had been approved. I was allowed twenty persons on my list so I wanted it full, because even if you had twenty people on your list, the chances of lots of visits were small. The more people, the better the chances for visits. I loved visits and I wanted all I could get.

Sandy had been approved to visit for over a month and she still hadn't told me for sure if she was ever going to visit. I knew she had a new relationship, so one time while I was talking to her I told her I understood if she couldn't come to visit and I would take her name off my list. She said, "Don't take it off just yet. Give me another two weeks. Okay?"

A month after Sandy had asked me to give her another two weeks to make up her mind, I was walking the corridor nervously waiting for her to arrive for a visit. Finally, late that afternoon, I heard my name called for a visit. I hurried to get to the visiting room. Sandy was standing just inside the visiting room area where the vending machines were located. I felt so silly because I didn't know what to do or say. So I just kissed her on the lips. She didn't pull back, but she kissed me back.

We both smiled and walked into the visiting room seating area and found a place to visit. She looked me dead in the eyes and said, "What am I going to do with you?" We both laughed, but those words stuck in my mind.

We had such a wonderful time visiting. We were still talking a mile a minute when they announced that visiting hours were over.

Sandy was a divorced mother of a six-year-old son named Blake. I had never met him, but I knew he was her pride and joy. I had seen pictures of him and he was a very handsome, well developed young man. I knew she was a very good mother by all the things she was always doing with him.

Sandy came to see me again around Christmas. Again we had a wonderful time. We were always so relaxed with each other. The time seemed to fly because we were never at a loss for words. Sandy told me she had decided to break off her current relationship because she couldn't see both of us at the same time. I told her I would really like to see her more if possible. She said, "How about once a month?" I said, "How about once a week?" We laughed and finally we agreed on twice a month. That was quite a bit considering the drive and the cost.

We visited for the next four months and every visit was exciting. Every time she came to see me she looked like a million dollars. Other inmates continually remarked about how attractive she was. Not only that, but at the camp we were allowed to attend church together at the chapel on Sunday. Our visits went so fast it seemed like the whole weekend was over in just hours.

One visit, I was just sitting there listening to Sandy tell me about what she had done the past two weeks at home. I was almost hypnotized as I gazed deep into her crystal clear blue eyes. I noticed her beautiful smile and how I loved to hear her laugh and how good she smelled. Then, just like I was hit over the head with a hammer, I fell instantly in love with her. I mean hopelessly in love! I felt like someone poured warm honey all over my body. It was a definite warm and fuzzy feeling. It was like God opened a special set of eyes that I had never been able to see through before. When He opened these eyes I realized I was looking at the answer to my prayer. It was her all the time, but I was too blind to see!

Or was I too blind to see? Was it just God's wisdom that wouldn't let me see until certain things could take place?

During the past five months, Sandy and I had developed a deep relationship as best friends. We had been able to talk for hours and days without any distractions or interruptions. We were able to know each other in a way most people never get to do. We had taken the time to listen and learn about each other. We found out that we had hundreds of things in common and we were in agreement about most things. We had developed a foundation that would make us best friends first and pave the way for a lasting relationship.

We were like high school sweethearts and best friends all rolled into one. I fell head over heels in love with my best friend. I didn't feel like

I had to guard my heart any longer. I felt like it belonged to her anyway and she should have it.

I also realized that until I had established a personal relationship with God, I had been totally unable to love someone this way. I had always guarded a part of my heart and could never give myself totally to anyone. I had a real problem in this way. I could give ninety percent, but I could never let the other ten percent out of my possession. For the first time in my life, the Lord allowed me to love in a way that I was meant to love. It had taken the Lord three-and-a-half years in prison to break down the wall I had surrounded myself with stemming from the pain and hurt I had suffered as a child. Then He brought me to the place where I could love with all my heart.

As I looked into Sandy's sparkling blue eyes I could feel the fireworks. As I looked into the eyes of God's perfect mate for me, I knew without a doubt this was the one.

The question now was—did Sandy know that I was God's perfect mate for her? Did she feel the same fireworks in her heart? Was I the one for her too?

CHAPTER 13

Something Is Terribly Wrong!

With the faith and trust of a child, I told Sandy exactly how I felt. I was trusting that God had given her the same love for me as I had for her. I was even able to say sweet, romantic things to her that I could have never said before. She told me that she felt the same way and that she loved me deeply. Yes! Yes! Yes! My spirit soared and my heart swelled to hear that this beautiful woman, and my best friend, loved me as much as I loved her.

We continued to visit every other week, but she started coming on Friday so we could visit Friday evening, Saturday day, and Sunday day. We also started to talk on the phone for a few minutes every night. Our romance was on fire despite the fact we only saw each other every two weeks in the visiting room.

About two months after I told Sandy I loved her, I developed a physical problem. I was lifting weights at the iron pile one day with a friend. We were doing our regular routine; nothing new or extreme.

While I was doing an incline bench press, I felt a sharp pain around my right shoulder blade. I was sure I had severely pulled or torn a muscle. Within an hour the first two fingers on my right hand began to lose feeling. I prepared an ice pack and lay on my bed with the ice trying to ease the pain. Even the next night, it was still killing me. I thought about missing my college class because my arm and shoulder hurt so badly. But I went to class and asked the professor if I could just lie on the floor and listen because I was in too much pain to take notes.

I worked for the Camp Hospital at this time, but when I went to sick call and told the PA what had happened, he still wouldn't give me anything for pain. Instead, he gave me some anti-inflammatories that made my stomach upset all the time.

A month later it was still hurting, so when the orthopedic surgeon came to the camp to see some other inmates, the PA asked him if he could take a look at me. He examined me and measured my right arm and shoulder and found that I had lost some size on my upper right side. He gave me two shots near my right shoulder blade and the pain finally subsided.

I had taken off some time from lifting weights, but when I went back my right side was still very weak. I began to experience more weakness, muscle loss, and weight loss, along with the loss of feeling in my right hand. I noticed I was also losing part of my upper arm, forearm, chest, and back muscles on my right upper side.

Despite all these physical problems, Sandy and I were still floating on a cloud. We seemed to fall in love more each day. I began to think more and more about marriage, but even still this was an area that was difficult for me to approach. Even though I had prayed to God specifically to bring me a wife, the more I thought about marriage, the more afraid I became.

I remember I began to look up scriptures about marriage and a wife. I wanted to see what God had to say about marriage. The more I read, the more I realized that God held marriage as a sacred institution. One of my favorite scriptures came from Proverbs: "He who finds a wife finds a good thing, and obtains favor from the LORD" (Proverbs 18:22). I couldn't imagine. The Lord actually shows favor to those who are married.

This was something new to me. I had been single all my life and actually poked fun at my friends if they even suggested they were getting married. I had intentionally, without knowing, made fun of God's vow to show favor to those who marry. As I searched His Word, I realized how wrong I had been.

I loved Sandy so much. I had already said she deserved better than me, but could I be the godly husband and father that Sandy deserved if she were to agree to marry me? I was scared. I had come to realize the tremendous responsibilities that a man is accountable to God for when he asks for the hand of a woman in marriage. I was scared that I might let her down and God. I knew the Lord loved Sandy just as much as He did me, so I had to be as special to her as she was to me.

At this time Sandy and I had made a prayer list and every Friday we fasted and then at 5:30 A.M. every Saturday morning we prayed at the same time. We prayed for family, friends, and even people we didn't know. I remember the incredible feeling I had every time I prayed knowing we were praying in agreement at the same time even though we were in separate locations. I would imagine I was kneeling side by side with Sandy before the throne of God. I'd never done anything like this before, and I felt like a new man every time we prayed together.

One time when I was praying at the Chapel alter I decided to take my situation before the Lord, I told the Lord that I wanted Sandy with all my heart. I remember I felt a peace come over me and I started weeping before the Lord. I wept for the longest time and then, when I was finished praying, I knew in my heart that the Lord had broken all the strongholds that had come against me to keep me from marrying. I knew the Lord had accepted my vow for Sandy. I knew she was going to be my wife, but did she?

It was only two weeks before her birthday. I planned and rehearsed how I would ask her to marry me. I didn't have many options considering I had to ask her during a visit and I couldn't get on my knees or anything romantic like that. I couldn't even offer her a ring. It just so happened that Sandy was coming to visit on her birthday.

It would be a perfect time to ask her to marry me. I was scared. What if she said no or she had to think about it? No, I couldn't think like that because I was sure the Lord had showed me that she was the one.

I remember seeing some of my Christian inmate friends through the visiting room window on the day of her birthday. They were trying to inconspicuously ask me if I had popped the question yet. They all knew about it because it was all I could talk about.

Finally, I got up enough nerve and asked her if she would marry me. She said, "Yes!" When she did, I thought I would float out of the room. I was so proud and so in love. She was wearing a beautiful black dress with white trim, so I asked the photographer to take a picture of her so I would have that memory forever. I was now engaged to be married. This was July, 1994.

Soon after this I was called out of the Camp for a special medical test. I went downtown Terre Haute, Indiana, to an MRI Center. I was loaded into the cylinder and they ran a MRI scan on my neck.

About a week later I was called to medical to get my results. The diagnosis was that I had a Classic C-7. This meant that between vertebras six and seven in my neck, I had a bulging disc that was causing nerve pressure, that in turn was causing my problems. They said I would be sent to Rochester Federal Medical Prison (for the fourth time) for a minor surgery to correct the problem and I would be back in a couple of months.

Wow! What great news. Sandy and I were relieved to hear that this could be corrected with minor surgery. In the meantime, we had a wonderful summer falling even deeper in love. We weren't concerned in the least. Even though I had lost about twenty pounds of muscle, we were sure I would get it all back as soon as the pressure was taken off the nerves.

Since we were now engaged, Sandy and I agreed that it was time I meet her six-year- old son, Blake. We wanted to plan a fun trip and not make him have to stay the whole day in the visiting room if he didn't want to. I talked to my brother and he was willing to come along on the visit and if Blake didn't want to stay the whole day, he could take him to the motel.

We got a motel with a swimming pool because we knew Blake loved to swim. On the first day we had a wonderful time. He was very shy at first, but he warmed up as the day wore on. Each day we let him have the option to go back to the room for the last two hours of visiting with my brother or stay with us. Each day he opted to swim. Let's face it, that's a lot of competition. But not long after his visit, he sent me a wonderful letter. I still treasure this letter and I want to share it with you just as he wrote it:

Dear Dany I had a relly
fun time att the camp
last week and I wat to
come back some. I had
a relay good time at the
hotel and I Love wou
veory much you can
tak that to the Bank
Love Blazer P.S I miss
you veary much
todad y

I had gotten my answer from the Lord that Sandy was the one for me. But as the next few weeks passed, Sandy shared her feelings with me that she was concerned about the remaining time I had left to serve.

I had to do the time regardless, but she didn't have to. Shortly after she told me she was a little worried about my remaining time, I called her on the phone one evening. As soon as she answered, she was bubbling over with joy. She said she had something very special to tell me that night and she was so glad it was me calling. She said she had been praying fervently to God about our engagement and future marriage. She needed a confirmation from God to know what she should do. As she was deep in prayer she received a revelation from God. A warm feeling came over her and in her spirit she knew that she couldn't do the time, but He could and would do it for her if she would only let Him. She put her trust in the Lord to do it for her and had total peace from that moment on. After she told me about her revelation, I whispered a silent "thanks" to the Lord.

We were both crazy in love and we had both received a confirmation from God during prayer so we decided not to wait any longer to marry. We decided to get married before I was transferred to a Medical Prison for surgery. We put in a request to staff to begin the necessary arrangements. Now it was just a matter of time before Sandy would be my wife.

While we were waiting I decided to start researching my legal possibilities to try to get a sentence reduction. I went back to my transcripts and I came up with an angle.

The lab reports on the cocaine that I sold came back with a reading of twenty-nine percent purity. That meant that seventy percent of the ingredients were not an illegal substance. The cocaine was so weak that less than one-third of it was cocaine. When I figured out the actual weight of the cocaine I sold, I realized that I had only sold enough to warrant a five-year sentence. If I could win a motion in court, I would be home in a year. I got some help from the friend of a friend and filed a motion in court.

Sandy and I were ecstatic about the possibility that I could be released in a year. Things were looking good. I could get this minor surgery out of the way, then maybe home soon after that.

I started to research the Scriptures for everything I could find about marriage so that I could write our vows. This was one of the most exciting things I had ever done—looking through God's Word to find words to use for our marriage. I wanted to do everything God's way. No more my way or the highway stuff. I loved God and I knew He had truly answered my prayer for a wife.

During this time Sandy sent me a book called *Becoming One* by Don Meredith. I couldn't believe the things I learned from this book. I began to realize that marriage is something more special and intimate than anything I had ever imagined. How every man and woman was to become one in marriage. That both were incomplete without the other and together they could become one. Wow! I'd never heard about this before. I devoured the book. I loved how I felt and all that the Lord was teaching me. I could see God now working through Sandy too.

I daily poured over Scripture to find just the right words for our vows. Then one night I remember having the most incredible dream. In my dream I remember looking through my eyes and everything was bright and shiny and new. Quickly, I realized that Sandy and I were looking out of the same eyes. I could feel that we were entwined together. Every fiber of my body was in her body and every fiber of her body was in mine. We were woven together. Not only physically, but we were in perfect harmony in spirit. We were in perfect agreement. If I wanted to go right, she wanted to go right and if she wanted to go left, I wanted to go left too. We flowed together as one.

As I was saturated with this feeling of love for Sandy, the thought came to me that the way I felt was the same way that God felt. That the Father, Son, and Holy Spirit were in perfect harmony and always in perfect agreement, and that marriage is a shadow of the mystery of the Holy Trinity. Three distinct personalities that are one, just as Sandy and I were to become one.

When I woke up I actually had tears in my eyes. The dream made me so happy that I cried as I slept. I couldn't wait to tell Sandy. It was the most wonderful dream that I could ever imagine.

Then I was taken from the prison, by surprise, for another test to downtown Terre Haute at Regional Hospital. This one was called an EMG and it was performed by a neurologist. It consists of a series of electrical shocks and needles pushed into your muscles to check your nerve conduction to determine whether or not disease is present. I remember the doctor did something he said he hadn't done in years. He stuck one of the needles into my tongue. The doctor didn't tell me the findings of his tests. He simply said he would make a report and send it to my doctor in the Camp.

About a week after the EMG, which was then September 7, 1994, and before we could get married, I was called to pack up my property and prepare to leave. When I took my property to the guard, he told me I was going to Springfield, Missouri, Federal Medical Prison that day. I told him that he was mistaken because I was going to Rochester, Minnesota, Federal Medical Prison. He assured me I was going to Springfield.

That afternoon, I was taken to a private airfield and flown directly to Springfield, Missouri, by a six-passenger jet. Believe me, this was not the type of transportation I was accustomed to. Something was wrong. Terribly wrong.

At Springfield I was put under the care of the chief neurologist Dr. Klinkerfuss. At the time I didn't know it, but Dr. Klinkerfuss was a former Assistant Director of Washington University School of Medicine (Division of Neurology) at Barnes Hospital, St. Louis, Missouri. Barnes Hospital is one of the finest in the world. This would soon prove to be a curse and a blessing.

For the next two weeks I underwent a battery of tests. Then, on September 28, 1994, I was called to Dr. Klinkerfuss's office. Dr. Klinkerfuss is a soft-spoken man. He is very professional and thorough. He told me he had run so many tests because he was trying to rule out everything he could before he made his final diagnosis. I was ready to get the surgery over with and get back to the camp and be with Sandy. I thought to myself—I wish he would just set a date for the neck surgery and get on with it!

However, he didn't say anything about surgery and told me that I was misdiagnosed about a pinched nerve in my neck. In fact, he told me he had some very distressing news and that maybe I should sit first. Then he proceeded to tell me I had a terminal disease called Amyotropic Lateral Sclerosis or ALS, better known as Lou Gehrig's disease. He said there was no cure and the only known treatment was in the experimental stage. He said it was against the Federal law for an inmate (or a member of the armed forces) to take experimental medicine. He also told me that because I had suffered so much damage during the past months, I might only have a year or two to live. This is a copy of Dr. Klinkerfuss's diagnosis:

U.S. MEDICAL CENTER FOR FEDERAL PRISONERS
SPRINGFIELD, MISSOURI

Special Progress Note

COX, Danny
Reg. No. 22427-044
28 September 1994

Mr. Cox was admitted to this institution for a putative cervical disc which is of no clinical significance. However, he has generalized fibrillations and fasciculations in EMG and clinically he has giant motor units in his left trapezius with wasting of the right trapezius and fasciculations in this area clinically. His diagnosis is amyotrophic lateral sclerosis or another name is motor systems disease. It is commonly known Lou Gehrig's disease. The course of this illness is of progressive muscle wasting and weakness leading to death. There is no standard treatment; however, there are several experimental studies going on across the United States. The one at Mayo Clinic, which is the only one available within the Bureau of Prison system, is full at this point and he is not a candidate for treatment in that group. Since without treatment the prognosis is very poor, this man should be considered for compassionate release so he can seek treatment for his condition. I cannot predict accurately how rapidly his disease will progress but in the last year it has progressed significantly.

George H. Klinkerfuss, M.D.
Neurologist

GHK/dt
D&T: 09-28-94

Lou Gehrig's disease is a ruthless killer that attacks and kills the nervous system. As the nerve cells die, your muscles begin to waste away. At first your grip weakens and you begin to drop things. Then you begin to lose your balance and fall frequently. Then you need the support of a cane to walk. Next crutches, then you are bound to a wheelchair. You become weaker and weaker until someone has to feed you, bathe you, and change your clothes. Finally, you become so weak that you either choke to death trying to swallow your food or you suffocate because you don't even have enough strength to breathe. And all this time your mind is perfectly intact, trapped inside a prison of dying flesh.

When I left Dr. Klinkerfuss's office I was stunned. I felt like my mind and body were no longer connected. I was out of sync and couldn't collect my thoughts. This couldn't possibly be happening because the Lord had just given Sandy and me to each other for marriage and the only reason we weren't already married was we didn't have time before I was transferred from Terre Haute Prison to this medical prison.

I went back to my cell. There were people all around, but everything seemed to be in a fog. Nothing made sense. I cried out to God in my heart, *Why, Lord? Is this some kind of a cruel joke? I only came here for minor surgery to trim a bulging disc in my neck and go straight back to the camp. I'm supposed to gain back all the muscle I lost, marry Sandy, win my motion for a sentence reduction, and be home in about a year. I didn't come here to die.*

In 1991 and 1992 I had been an inmate volunteer at Rochester Federal Medical Prison. I was present when men died a cruel death in prison. I knew that the only thing worse than "being in prison" was "to die in prison."

Now it was me who was dying in prison.

Oh, God! How was I going to tell Sandy!

CHAPTER 14

Denied!

In the past, Sandy had worked for a doctors' group. Through her job she was very familiar with many medical terms and medical procedures as well as diseases. At this particular time, she was working for a Physical Rehab Clinic.

She was a medical secretary, plus she had several other responsibilities which caused her to have contact with the patients. I remember when I had been diagnosed with the Classic C-7, she found a man in the Clinic who had just had an operation to correct a C-7 problem. She asked him if he would tell her about it because her fiancé had the same problem.

The man told her that his surgery was minor and that they went into his neck from the front and trimmed away the bulging parts between the discs. Just six weeks after his surgery, he was already in Rehab and was getting back the feeling in his fingers and his strength was improving daily. Sandy was the kind of person who liked to know the facts. She had already told me all about the conversation with this man and we both felt confident I would recover just as quickly as he had, if not quicker.

But now, the whole picture had changed. Exactly three weeks to the day after I had been flown to Springfield, I was now diagnosed with a deadly disease. It was no longer a situation of a simple corrective surgery, but how long I would live.

As I walked down the hall to the telephone, I felt so hollow inside. I knew that I had to call Sandy, but I didn't want to. I had just received the most incredible love letter from her the night before and she was preparing to come to Springfield the next weekend to see me. The letter was full of encouragement and she told me she couldn't wait for me to get back to the camp to get married.

I usually didn't call Sandy at work because she was always busy. So when she picked up the phone in the middle of the afternoon, she was surprised that it was me.

Even still her voice was as sweet as honey, which made the situation a lot more difficult if that were possible. It didn't take her long though to detect something was wrong. I just couldn't hide my emotions well that day.

I told her the story from the very beginning. When I got to the part about Lou Gehrig's disease, it must have been one of the few diseases that she was not familiar with. But then she asked me what it was and I described it to her as it was described to me by the doctor. There was silence first, then a burst of tears and sobbing. We both just hung on the phone crying together. Neither of us could speak for a while. It was absolutely horrifying.

Then she asked me to hold. When she came back on the line she told me to call her at home in an hour. She had told her boss that an emergency had just come up and she couldn't work the rest of the day. He let her go home. Everybody at the Rehab Clinic was like family. They all looked out for each other. I knew that at the moment she hung up, her coworkers were right there to console her, but I didn't have anyone to comfort me. Yes, there were over a thousand other inmates there, but I was still alone, alone and scared.

In the meantime, I called my mother. She too was devastated. We had already been through so much and now this. My God, what else could happen? How far was this whole nightmare going to go? When would it end?

Just after I had gotten off the phone with my mother I called the lawyer who had helped me put together the motion for a sentence reduction, which had been filed the month prior and was still under consideration by the court. I told him the whole story and he told me that I had to get all of my medical records together as soon as possible and send him copies. In the meantime, he would begin to prepare an Emergency Motion to the judge pleading with him to resentence me to time served due to extreme medical circumstances that were unforeseen at the time of my original sentencing.

The lawyer had given me a spark of hope that at least I could tell Sandy I might be released soon. I was still in shock and all I could think about now was getting home quickly so that Sandy and I could go to some big healing ministry where the healing power of God had been known to flow to seek divine healing. After all, the doctor had made it perfectly clear that according to medical science, there was no cure on this earth. I had to get out of prison. I had to get out soon, before it was too late.

When I called Sandy at home she was a mess. Her voice was raspy and she was still crying. She too was so confused and hurt. She couldn't believe she had finally found the one man she was sure that God had meant for her and now I was going to be taken from her before we could ever be together.

I told her what the lawyer said and at least we had something to hang on to. In the meantime, she was going to make calls and try to find out everything she could about this terrifying disease. She couldn't rest until she knew all she could know. Her first move was to call an 800 number she got from someone at work.

So, for the next few days I did all I could from my end and rounded up the medical records and got them in the mail to my lawyer. There was nothing else I could do now except wait to see Sandy that weekend in the visiting room.

The visiting room procedures at Springfield were different than at all the other prisons where I had served time. When you reached the visiting room at Springfield, you were first searched, then stripped and made to wear a jumpsuit during your visit just like in a county jail. I was tall so I had to wear a 2x so it was long enough in the crotch. But this only made me look even thinner than I already was because the jumpsuit was almost as wide as it was long.

My weight loss hadn't made a difference before because we were so sure my problem was a Classic C-7. But now everything was different. Sandy noticed everything. She was now concerned about how thin I was. And the jumpsuit made matters even worse.

That first visit was bittersweet. We loved each other so much, but now we were struggling to survive. All we had to hang on to now was the possibility that the judge would reconsider my original sentence.

At the time of my sentencing, the judge had asked my lawyer if there was any reason that the sentence of 120 months should not be imposed on me. At the time my lawyer had no reason. But circumstances that were unforeseen then were apparent now.

I was a first-time, nonviolent offender. Surely this should have some bearing on the judge's decision. I had already served forty-one months with a perfect conduct record.

I now had two motions before the court, one asking for a reduction of the sentence due to the small percentage of cocaine that was actually present when it was sold and an Emergency Motion asking for the judge to reduce my sentence to time served due to the diagnosis and prognosis. If I won the Motion for time served, I would be released immediately to pursue the only source of treatment that was available, which was in the experimental stage. As a federal prisoner I was prohibited by law to take any experimental medicine, and the only treatment available was classified "experimental." So as long as I was a federal prisoner, I couldn't receive the same treatment that was available to everyone else who had ALS. At this point, being a prisoner kept me from being eligible to take a medicine that could possibly extend my life even if it was for only a short while.

As I thought about the seriousness of my circumstances, Galatians 6:7-8 came to my mind: "Do not be deceived, God is not mocked; for whatever a man sows, that he will also reap. For he who sows to his flesh will of the flesh reap corruption...." Then I thought back about the thirty years of sin in my life and the seeds of corruption that I had sown. God's law of sowing and reaping cannot be broken!

The lawyer was extremely fast and only eight days after we filed the Emergency Motion, the judge ruled on both motions. On October 9, 1994, the judge denied both motions! He said that even though the mixture was only thirty percent cocaine and seventy percent substances that were not illegal, because I represented the entire mixture as cocaine, I would be charged with the weight of the entire mixture. On the ruling of the Emergency Motion, the judge said that I needed to go through the Bureau of Prisons for my release remedy. I knew that the judge could have very easily let me go with the stroke of a pen. Again I said, *Why can't I go home, Lord? Why can't I just go home and be with Sandy in these last days?*

I was feeling despondent about my rejection from the courts and my diagnosis. At first, I even had a hard time going to worship services because I wasn't ready to talk about it to others yet.

However, after a short while, I decided to go to a Yokefellows Praise and Worship Service held at the chapel every Wednesday night. This was a group of about twenty volunteers from the Springfield area.

This group was comprised of retired pastors, Bible teachers, and other good Christian men and women. The presiding pastor had been coming to the prison for twenty-one years. This man had seen many men come and go in these years. Some were released and some were carried out in body bags. He was no stranger to death and disease at the prison. An average of about ten men a month died in the Springfield Medical Prison.

The Yokefellows would form a large circle in the middle of the Chapel. We were seated inmate, volunteer, inmate, volunteer and so on. This particular night I was feeling very low. I felt like I needed sympathy or at least that someone would know about the struggle I was going through. I was really mixed up. I wanted everyone to know, but at the same time, I didn't want to talk about it.

Near the end of the service the pastor went to the middle of the circle and asked if anyone needed prayer. I wanted to stand, but my legs felt like they weighed a ton. Finally, after what seemed like forever, I stood by my chair and the pastor acknowledged me and said, "What is your prayer request tonight, son?" With a trembling voice I said, "Pastor, I was just recently diagnosed with Lou Gehrig's disease and I want the Lord to heal me."

No sooner had the words left my mouth than I saw the tears begin to well in the pastor's eyes. He came toward me and when he reached me he wrapped his arms around me and wept on my shoulder. This man had seen it all and he knew that unless the Lord healed me, I would soon die a horrible death.

By this time many people were laying hands on me and crying with us. The pastor prayed a passionate prayer for my healing. After the prayer I wiped the tears from my eyes and began to believe God right then for my healing. After all, I had all these strong Christian men and women praying for me so God surely heard their prayers.

When the service was over, I walked into the lobby area to wait for the ten-minute controlled movement so I could return to my cell. While I was waiting, one of the Christian volunteers singled me out and said, "Danny, it's not always God's will to heal everybody, so don't get your hopes up. Okay?" Instantly I was crushed! What hope and faith I had just received vanished into thin air.

I knew that every one of these people were godly men and women and they probably all knew more about God and His Word than I did. I couldn't understand it. Why would they even pray for me like that if they didn't think God would heal me for sure? What would be the point? I thought it was God's will to heal everyone. Maybe it wasn't. Now I was confused again because I believed these people knew much more than I did about prayer and healing.

When I got back to my cell, I cried out to God, *What do You do, Lord? Flip a coin and heads Danny lives and tails he dies? Is there a Lottery in Heaven and I have to be the lucky number to live or what? What is the truth, Lord? What is it?*

But then I got mad and I became determined to find out the answer from God for myself. I wasn't going to trust anyone but God, because then and only then could I be sure. So I began to pray and seek God like never before. I began to read the Bible continually and memorize scripture. I had already studied the Bible for the past forty-three months, but I was still not sure about healing.

Soon after the judge denied my motion for immediate release, I was told by my doctor that, on my behalf, the staff had agreed to begin the paperwork for a compassionate release from prison. Instantly, Sandy and I received new hope. It wasn't over yet.

I had seen others get compassionate releases from Rochester Prison. A compassionate release was strictly a consideration for someone who had been diagnosed terminal and couldn't serve out their time as originally sentenced. But even if you were terminal, that didn't guarantee that you would be released.

There were other things involved like your past criminal history record and what your current charges were. If you were a violent criminal, you wouldn't have a chance to be released even if you were on your deathbed. Even if you did fit all the other criteria, you still had to have someone who would declare, in writing, that they would agree to care for you and they were economically able to do this. This was the major reason that Ted (from Rochester) couldn't go home and die in peace.

The Case Manager called me in to start the paperwork and asked me if I had someone to care for me, and I thanked God that Sandy wanted me to be with her. I was a first-time, nonviolent offender and I had someone who offered to care for me. So the case manager told me that when he received a letter stating that I had a caregiver, he would proceed with the paperwork. He also told me that this would take time and not to get in a hurry.

During this time I received great support from Sandy, my family and friends. Sandy even wanted to marry me there instead of waiting for my release. I couldn't wait. I may have been sick, but the fire in my heart for her hadn't changed one bit. I went to the staff and requested that they start the procedure for us to marry. But I was told we couldn't marry there because they didn't permit the license to be brought into the prison for me to sign and I wouldn't be permitted to go outside the prison to get it. Another bitter disappointment.

I was only allowed four visits a month in Springfield. This made matters worse because what I needed most was the love of Sandy and my family. I split the month into two weekends. Sandy came to visit every two weeks and once a month my family came to visit at the same time she visited. I was so grateful for the visits, but there was always a little tension in the air and that couldn't be avoided.

Sandy had called the National ALS Headquarters and they sent her a package in the mail about Lou Gehrig's. She wanted to know all she could about it. But when she got the package, she found it so depressing she finally had to throw it away. There was nothing good to say anywhere. No encouragement at all. The only thing they did was to show you what kind of equipment that was available to care for the victim as they went through the stages of debilitation to death.

Even still, Sandy was incredible. She never missed a visit and continually made sure I knew without a doubt she loved me—something I needed more than anything at the time. I did notice she had lost quite a bit of weight too. The stress and strain of the situation were very hard on her as well.

I had been living in a large bull-pen room with about fifteen men. It was so loud most of the time you could hardly hear yourself think. I remember the block guard came over to my bunk and told me that I was next on the waiting list for a one-man cell. Some men were transferred when their medical problems were solved and some died there. So you moved up the seniority list pretty fast. I could barely hear him above the noise when he asked me if I wanted the one-man cell. I said, "Daaaaaaa. Yeah, I want it!"

I'm sure it's great to have a million dollar home and the luxuries that come with that type of living, but to me that 6 foot x 10 foot private cell was like a penthouse apartment at Caesar's Palace. This was mid December 1994. Many times your cellmate didn't agree with you spiritually so this gave me the opportunity to read and pray and praise God out loud without disturbing anyone or being disturbed. I could walk back and forth praising God night and day.

I began to dig even deeper into God's Word to find the truth about healing. When I read the Bible I didn't just read a chapter or two, I read the whole book. For example, I would read the whole book of Matthew or Luke in a sitting. I read every book on healing, faith and miracles I could get my hands on.

I read Christian books by anointed Bible teachers to bring me to a better understanding of God's Word. I memorized more Scripture. I began to praise God and thank Him every day in all things. My faith was rising daily and I was even able to thank God when things didn't go the way I wanted them to go. I knew that I was in a life-and-death battle, but I had a tremendous will to live. And if it was God's will to heal me, then I was going to be healed.

Just before Christmas that year I was concerned about what to send Sandy for Christmas. Springfield had a very limited Christmas card giveaway through the chapel and I was very disappointed indeed. But the Lord has a way of providing even in the darkest situations.

A week before Christmas I was sitting in church on Sunday morning. Close to the end of the service words began to pour into my heart. The words began to take form. They began to rhyme and take on verse.

The words came faster and faster. I couldn't concentrate the last few minutes, so as soon as the service was over I went straight to my cell and began to write down the words that flowed through my heart. After I finished the poem that God gave me, my heart was touched. Tears welled in my eyes. The Lord had given me a special poem for Sandy. A Christmas poem. This poem is dear to my heart and I would like to share it with you at this time:

> To My Darling Sandy,
>
> Every year at Christmas
> gifts are given and received;

most are temporary, without thought,
this you can believe.
But a gift that comes from heaven
takes time and careful thought;
knit together by the King Himself
creates a gift that can't be bought.
My gift was already made
before I said my prayer,
to ask for a gift as precious as this
you know I would not dare.
You see, God in all His wisdom
has sent her from above.
He has given to me the one to be
my perfect gift of love!

Christmas came and went and then January rolled around. The staff at Springfield had been working on my compassionate release since October 1994 and finally, in January 1995, it was almost ready.

Dr. Klinkerfuss called me to his office and told me he wanted one more diagnosis to go along with the two he already had. So, I was taken downtown to Cox Hospital in Springfield, Missouri, to undergo another EMG. About a week after this second EMG, I was told that the diagnosis from the specialist at Cox Hospital was the same as the first EMG and Dr. Kinkerfuss's diagnosis. This was the final step to be completed for the request for a compassionate release. I now had three concurring diagnoses from three different doctors. The paperwork was finally complete.

The compassionate release was approved and signed by the Warden; then it was sent to the Regional Offices for approval. Two weeks later it was approved and signed by Regional and forwarded to Washington, D.C., for the final approval.

In mid February 1995, Washington denied my compassionate release. Dr. Mortisugu, the Medical Director for the Bureau of Prisons, said that my condition was too stable at the time and that when my condition worsened, they would reconsider. In other words, they wouldn't consider releasing me until I was crippled. This was denial #2. Again, I was totally stunned. But I wasn't going to give up. Never!

I knew I had to trust the Word of God like a little child, so even though I had been diagnosed terminal by four doctors now, denied a bond three times, denied a compassionate release two times and was unable to get married twice, I thanked God for my healing, for my release from prison, and for my wife. I know this sounds crazy and maybe even like I was in denial, but I had learned in Romans 4:17 that God tells us to call things that are not yet manifested as though they already were. I began to do just that. I didn't care what things looked like anymore. If God's Word said it, I believed it no matter what.

All this time I was as thin as a rail, losing my hair, losing my appetite, and experiencing fasciculations (muscles continuously jumping involuntarily) and one leg felt weaker than the other.

I absolutely dreaded to tell Sandy that I had been denied a release for a second time. I called her and told her and she cried from a broken heart. I knew this was getting harder and harder for her, but there was nothing I could do but trust God.

Then I was called to my Unit Manager's Office and he told me that the staff was very disappointed that my compassionate release was denied by Washington. He said the Warden was going to personally appeal on my behalf. I was told that once a compassionate release was denied at the national level, the inmate could no longer appeal. Only the Warden could intervene and he was going to. I was very excited.

Surely Washington wouldn't deny a direct appeal by the Warden. Praise God!

In my first year of incarceration (1991), I was a volunteer Hospice worker at Rochester, Minnesota, Federal Medical Prison. So I went to the chaplain there and told him of my prior experience and asked to be an inmate Hospice volunteer there. He made a call to the chaplain at Rochester and verified my prior training and work record, and I was accepted immediately.

Each Hospice volunteer is assigned an inmate patient who is chronic or terminal. At the time I was accepted, there were no terminal patients (that could speak English) that were not already covered by another inmate volunteer.

So while I was waiting for an assignment in Hospice, I decided to volunteer for another program called "PAL." Under PAL you were assigned to an inmate who needed assistance, but they were not terminally ill. These people generally needed someone to take them outside in a wheelchair so they could get some fresh air and sunshine.

In my case I was assigned to an inmate who had just had a mild stroke. He was undergoing therapy to learn to walk again after he suffered damage to his left leg and arm. His face was a little numb, but he could still talk okay. As far as I was concerned, as long as I could walk, I was going to help someone less fortunate.

The first week after I became a Hospice worker, another volunteer inmate was assigned to show me around floor two and three of Building 1. This Christian man's name was John McConnell, and he later turned out to be my best friend in Springfield. Then John took me to the floor to visit the man he was assigned to. I will never forget walking into this man's cell.

He was lying on his bunk with his wheelchair at the foot of his bunk. He was drawn into a slight fetal position. He didn't move or say anything to us when we entered the room, but his eyes followed our every move.

John smiled at the man on the bunk and with loving care he touched his shoulder and said, "Nick, I want you to meet our newest Hospice volunteer. His name is Danny and he has Lou Gehrig's too." His eyes stared at me knowingly, but he couldn't speak or make any expression.

John had been Nick's constant companion and friend for the past nine months. John had spent quality time with Nick every day and had been a personal witness to Nick's physical decline.

Like the close friend that John truly was to Nick, he spoke for Nick out of respect. He said, "Nick is unable to speak, Danny, but I'm sure he's glad to meet a friend of mine." I acknowledged and tried to force a smile and regain my composure. Even though I was believing God for my healing, it was all I could do to see firsthand the horrible, twisted, lifeless condition that ALS victims suffer before death.

After we left Nick's cell, John told me Nick couldn't move any body part except one foot slightly, his head barely and his eyes. He could barely swallow liquid and soft foods and he had to be spoon-fed.

As we walked and talked, it was all I could do to keep my knees from buckling. John told me they had designed a special electronic pad to lie under Nick's head. Nick had just enough strength left in his neck that he could press slightly and an alarm would sound in the nurses' station when he needed assistance.

Springfield Medical Prison is different than most prisons in that the buildings are arranged in a square. There is an underground tunnel (or corridors) connecting each one to the other. You can go to any building through the tunnel, then take an elevator up to the floor you wish.

After I met Nick, it seemed like every time I turned around I would see him in the tunnel being pushed by an inmate PAL while his Hospice worker, John, was at work. And every time I saw him his fixed stare seemed to pierce me. He knew that in just a short while I would be in the same condition as him. He knew that one by one my limbs would fall limp at my side like his. He knew only too well the horror associated with being a Lou Gehrig's victim. About a month after I met Nick, I was up on the floor where he lived visiting with my PAL assignment. I left Ron's cell to run some errands for him when I began talking to another man just down the hall from Nick.

This man was very nice and sometimes I stopped in to say "Hi". This particular night he was standing partially out of his cell and I stopped to chat for a moment. As we talked, the same old question came around. He wanted to know why I was there in Springfield. Of course I told him

I was there on a medical transfer and then the dreaded question followed, so I told him I had been diagnosed with Lou Gehrig's disease.

Just about this time we looked down the hall, and Nick, who had been sitting in a wheelchair in his room, rolled backwards slowly into the hallway. He had been waiting for someone to come and get him and grew impatient so he used the little strength he had left in one foot and caused the wheelchair to roll backwards into the hallway.

Nick was slumped over in his wheelchair with his head tilted to one side, and he was looking down towards us as we talked.

Without a thought, the man I was talking to said, "You know, Nick was just about in the same shape you are now when he came in only a year ago."

His words pierced me like a dagger. I felt fear grip me with more force than I had ever felt. Nick was doing pretty good only one year ago. If this scenario was to be repeated in my case, I only had about nine months before I would be an invalid too. I had to get away from there fast and collect my thoughts. I excused myself and quickly left. To my knowledge Nick and I were the only two men in the entire Federal Prison System of over 100,000 inmates who had ALS. Nick died two weeks later and then it was just me!

CHAPTER 15

I Believe in Miracles

While I was waiting for the Warden's Appeal, I received the book, *How to Live and Not Die*[4] from Janice Kadell, a Christian friend. The book was written by Norvel Hayes, an anointed Bible teacher.

This book was written for someone like me—someone who was dying from a terminal disease. Brother Hayes doesn't mess around. He gets right down to business. He tells you step-by-step how to get healing from God. He doesn't compromise. He teaches healing straight from the Scripture. His book gave me more courage than ever. He told of a woman who had come to him dying of cancer with only a few months to live. Her doctors told her to go on home from the hospital and spend her last days at home because there was nothing more they could do for her.

As he teaches through the book, he tells the story of this how this frail little woman received her healing from God. I read the book and then I read it again and again. I couldn't read it enough. Every time I read it, my faith soared and I knew that if this little lady who was skin and bones, with no hair and only a couple of months to live, could receive her healing, then so could I.

I even wrote to Brother Hayes and told him about my situation. He wrote back a two-page letter of encouragement. He also said a special

---

[4] Norvel Hayes, *How to Live and Not Die* (Harrison House, 1986).

prayer for me in the letter. I was getting even more determined every day, and I had picked healing scriptures to stand on.

I had now memorized close to 100 scriptures, but Brother Norvel Hayes was adamant about the fact that I only needed one of God's scriptures to get my healing. One word from God had the power to move mountains, he said. I was also receiving free books and Bible studies from the Kenneth Copeland Prison Ministries. Sometimes I could catch Brother Copeland on TV at 5:30 in the morning. What a blessing his ministry is to the inmates.

Day by day I continued to believe God for my healing. I was sure now that God could heal me, and all I needed was to be sure He would.

Three weeks after the Warden had appealed the denial of my compassionate release, I was told that Washington had also denied the Warden's Appeal. This was now the third time that I had been denied release. Although this was harder for me to take than you can imagine, I dreaded telling Sandy more than anything. How much longer could she endure this kind of pain and continual letdowns? With all the strength I could muster, I thanked God for my release from prison, for healing me and for my wife.

This was now February 1995 and I had been in Springfield seven months already. Sandy had been there every other weekend faithfully and helped to encourage me. But what now? After all these denials could she hold up? I was now beginning to fear losing her. I knew that this was such an impossible situation from a physical point of view. I was trusting God, but not everyone had the faith I did. She was no doubt suffering a great deal from this whole ordeal. Maybe more than I would ever know.

On the day I was diagnosed terminal, I asked the doctor how much time I had left. He said I had suffered a lot of damage in the last year and from that he thought not long.

You never know how you will react to something like this. You see it in the movies and you read about it in books, but no matter how deeply you feel, it's almost impossible to put yourself in their shoes. It is always them and not you.

I do remember I was almost numb. I must have been in shock at the time of my diagnosis because I wasn't afraid. When I left the doctor's office I went to a phone. I wanted to call Sandy to tell her. I guess I was looking for comfort, but in a situation like this, your comfort is another's pain. There is just no way around it. When I told Sandy what the doctor said, she broke down, then I broke down with her. It completely devastated her and my family.

Then I got scared. I had so many questions and no answers. I had been going to church regularly for the past four years and I regularly attended weekly Bible studies. Still, I didn't know what to do. I thought I knew the Bible better than most and I did have a good understanding of the chronological order of events of history, but obviously I didn't know it well enough to draw on it in a time of crisis.

I was desperate. I had been praying to God for answers. I needed help and I was isolated behind the prison walls away from my family and friends and loved ones. I needed them. I needed their love in the most difficult circumstance that I had ever faced. I felt so alone, but I didn't realize that the One who made me was with me and wouldn't leave me. Not in prison, not anywhere!

While I was trusting God and believing for a miracle, for some unexplained reason, I allowed myself to stray from the Word of God for a moment. One day another volunteer Hospice worker that was Buddhist told me I should go down to the Education Department and listen to some tapes on healing. You will notice the healing tapes were not in the Chapel, but in the Education Department.

Of course, my belief is completely different than that of the Buddhist philosophy, but I was desperate and desperate men do desperate things. I am just thankful to God that He is able to give us light even when we search in total darkness.

I went down to the Education Department and I found the healing tapes. There were a variety of audio cassettes from many different religious disciplines. There were a lot of Eastern Mysticism tapes. I had no idea what to base my selection on, but finally a tape series by Dr. Stevens caught my eye.

The audio cassettes revealed that Dr. Stevens had been a cancer specialist in his early years, but had ventured into the field of healing through psychology. Stevens had a particular fascination with why, given the fact that all circumstances were equal in the cancer patients, some would get well and some would die after receiving the same treatment and medications. He decided to make this his life's work: to find out what was the deciding factor that made some live and some die.

At the time of the tapes, Stevens had been researching this phenomenon for about twenty years. He found that, besides medicine, our attitudes and beliefs have a profound effect on health and sickness. Stevens even quoted Plato as saying, "To treat the body without treating the mind is folly."

Stevens pointed out that our first line of defense against disease in our immune system. Our immune system is in our blood and our white blood cells, in particular, fight disease.

Our white blood cells can be affected in two ways, indirectly and directly. Our bodies can fight disease indirectly through the endocrine system by a direct release of chemicals into our bloodstream. This is a result of primarily three things: food intake, rest and exercise.

Our immune system is directly affected by our emotions, such as love, hate, anger, unforgiveness, joy, fear, depression, etc.

In 1984 it was discovered that every white blood cell has a built-in neuroreceptor. Instant messages from the brain are transmitted directly to the white blood cells. So, according to Dr. Stevens, our immune system, which is in the blood, and our first line of defense, is affected in a positive or negative manner by our emotions. As I listened to the recordings by Stevens, my inner thoughts reminded me that the Bible says in Leviticus 17:14 that our life is in our blood.

God says that our life is in our blood! We all know that life-giving oxygen and nutrients are carried by the blood to every cell and organ in our body. It's a fact that the loss of too much blood will cause certain death. Our blood also carries a built-in defense mechanism through our white blood cells. And, according to Stevens, our first line of defense is instantly affected by how we feel.

Dr. Stevens talked about a group of women who underwent chemotherapy for cancer in a blind test. In a blind test, half of the participants take the actual medicine being tested and the other half take a placebo (an inactive substance used as a control in an experiment). None of the participants were aware whether they were taking the real medication or the placebo. However, each one individually believed that they were taking the real medicine.

In the placebo group (those who were not actually taking any medication but thought they were taking chemotherapy), an incredible event took place. It's a well-known fact that cancer patients taking chemotherapy lose all of their hair. In the placebo group, thirty percent of the women lost all of their hair.

These women in the placebo group believed so deeply that they were taking the chemotherapy they actually produced the same side effects as the women who were actually taking the chemotherapy were experiencing.

Dr. Stevens made this statement: "Within one's mind there is a power capable of exerting forces which can either enhance or inhibit the process of disease."

I'm not certain if I originally approached the secular healing tapes actually thinking I would find a cure for an incurable disease or that I just needed to prove to myself that there was no cure for an incurable disease except through God.

As I reviewed the tape series, the Lord spoke to me in my spirit. He told me that Dr. Stevens didn't write the original book on healing, He did. He told me to look in His Word and He would show me the answer.

Doctors cannot heal. They are instruments of healing whom God has placed in our midst. We are born with the capacity to heal ourselves. Certain medicines and therapies help the body to heal faster, but the healing itself is a gift of God and a mystery to everyone including the medical profession. The Word of God is clear in Exodus 15:26, "For I am the Lord who heals you."

I began to search the Scriptures to find passages that dealt with words that described the emotions such as fear, love, unforgiveness, and complaining. Sure enough, everywhere I looked I found scriptures concerning these emotions. I found that God tells us over and over not to fear and not to doubt His Word, not to complain and not to hate. He even tells us to love our enemies. I couldn't believe I had missed this before. The answer was right in front of my eyes.

Negative emotions are not of God. He does not give us fear or doubt. Second Timothy 1:7 says, "For God has not given us a spirit of fear, but of power and of love and of a sound mind." You see, negative fears and doubts turn our thoughts away from God—our only source of healing.

The Bible makes it clear that when you take your eyes off of the Lord and focus on your circumstances, you look away from the source of your deliverance. When you focus on fear and doubt, you keep your eyes on the problem instead of the solution. God knows that when we let negative emotions rule our minds, we will lose whatever battle we are in.

If you are terminal with an incurable disease, you must keep your eyes on God. Focus on His power and love. Trust Him like a little child.

Even though I had looked in the wrong place, the Lord still taught me a valuable lesson, one that I wouldn't forget. After this lesson, I was ready to believe His Word above all. Dr. Stevens thought he discovered something new in his research, but the Word of God says in Ecclesiastes 1:9, "There is nothing new under the sun." What the doctor thought he discovered from years of research and tests, has been in the Bible for centuries. One only has to approach God like a little child and ask for wisdom to receive it according to James 1:5.

The Lord had another surprise for me. I went to the Chapel to look for a book to read. At the time I wasn't sure what book I was looking for, but I knew for sure that I was looking for one.

The Chapel library was very small and similar in size to a small child's bedroom. I would guess it to be about a 9 foot x 10 foot room. One of the longer walls was set up with a large screen TV for viewing spiritual videos and the other had wall-to-wall bookcases. The books were generally softbacks, but there were some hardbacks.

I stood before the books staring aimlessly and I realized that I didn't know what I was looking for. So I said a short prayer and asked God to direct me to the book He wanted me to read. Then I proceeded to search expectantly to find the right one. God is interested in small things in your life just as much as He is the big things.

My eyes began to focus on titles and authors and even colors. Suddenly, I saw the name "Kathryn Kuhlman." I remembered about her in the book, *Good Morning Holy Spirit*, by Benny Hinn. It had been one of the first books I had read after I rededicated my life to the Lord in the county jail. Sandy had sent it to me as a gift. Pastor Hinn had talked about the incredible anointed healing ministry that the Lord had given to Kathyrn Kuhlman. I knew instantly that this was the one.

I pulled out the paperback called *I Believe in Miracles*[5] and took it back to my cell with excitement in every step. I couldn't wait to read what the Lord had picked out for me. Was I in for a surprise!

The book itself was filled with miracle healings that had taken place during the Kuhlman Ministry. Not only was there a thorough description

[5]   Kathryn Kuhlman, *I Believe in Miracles, Revised Ed.* (Bridge Publishsers, 1992).

of each healing, but her staff had followed up on each case with a background on each person before and after the miracle healing. The details were right down to the name and city where they lived. No secrets or gray areas with her.

Tears of joy streamed down my cheeks as I read about each miracle healing. My spirit soared and I praised God for His love and mercy. I could feel waves of the Holy Spirit washing over my body from head to toe and goose bumps everywhere as my spirit witnessed the power of God through each and every story. An incredible hope was welling up, like a tidal wave, on the inside of me.

Then, there it was! A case of a woman who had been struck with Lou Gehrig's disease—the same devastating disease that I had been diagnosed with only a few months earlier. My heart skipped a beat.

The Mississippi River is a natural barrier between Missouri and Illinois. St. Louis, Missouri, sits right on the west bank of the river and extends westward. My hometown, Collinsville, Illinois, is on the east side of the river just ten miles from downtown St. Louis.

Kathryn Kuhlman was holding a meeting downtown St. Louis in the early 1950's. The place was packed with people who needed miracle healings and with thousands who had come to pray for others and to witness firsthand the healing power of God.

As I read there was a lump in my throat. The story was about a woman who lived in a small town that adjoined the northern border of Collinsville. The population was only about 2,500. Could this be? The woman in this book lived about three miles from where I was from.

Her name was Doris Hoffmeier. Doris had been struck with the deadly Lou Gehrig's disease. She was in the advanced stages and confined to a wheelchair. Her family had heard that Kathryn Kuhlman was coming to St. Louis and decided to take Doris to her meeting.

During the meeting, Kathryn called to this woman and told her to come up front. Doris was rolled up front. Kuhlman's attendants lifted Doris up and laid her on the stage. As Kathryn prayed for her, Doris looked up and said, "I can see Jesus sitting up in the corner of the roof." She began to praise God and her body was healed instantly. She sat up and walked away a healed woman. As I read the story I cried like a baby. The tears ran freely as if they were even washing my soul. The emotions I felt were incredible. I laid there for quite some time reflecting on the glory of God. I was content for my thoughts to just dwell on my Creator.

Then it dawned on me that I had to tell Sandy! I was beside myself with joy. I ran hurriedly to the phone and told her the whole story. She was not quite as excited about it as I was. Sandy wanted to believe, but she needed something more concrete to believe. She asked me the name of the woman again, so I gave her the name.

She knew as well as everyone that there was no cure for Lou Gehrig's. Lou Gehrig's is a death sentence. After I got off the phone I was a little let down, but I continued to cling to this miracle and claim my victory just like Doris had.

A few days passed and I called Sandy to say "Hi" and tell her I loved her as usual. When she answered she was all excited like I was the first time I had called and told her about Doris's miracle healing. Little did I know, but she had written down Doris' name and decided to do a little homework herself.

She told me she needed more proof than me so she started searching the phone book for Doris's number. She said, "After all, the book said that Doris lives just three miles from here, didn't it?" I couldn't argue with that. So then, if the book is true she should be able to verify the story by talking to Doris herself.

Sandy looked through the phone book and found the number for the Hoffmeier residence. She called and got in touch with Doris's grandson. She told him the whole story about what the book said and asked if she could talk to Doris to verify the story.

Doris's grandson told her that the story was true, but Doris had passed away a few years back from natural causes. Doris had been healed in the early 1950's and this was 1995. He told her that everything that was written was absolutely true and that God had indeed healed Doris from the incurable disease.

Sandy was now convinced. She knew God had already healed someone else from this dreadful disease, but would He heal me? What are the chances of finding a book like this by coincidence? A woman getting healed from Lou Gehrig's disease who lived only three miles from us? And her family name was still listed in the directory all these years?

This story turned out to be a miracle that was meant for both Sandy and me, to help me build on my faith and to give her new faith. Praise the Lord! And isn't it ironic that Sandy was the one who sent me the book *Good Morning Holy Spirit* that introduced me to the name of Kathryn Kuhlman for the first time?

Someone once said, "Coincidence is simply God's way of anonymously performing miracles!"

CHAPTER 16

Like a Bolt of Lightning

Even though so many things had changed in the past few months, Sandy and I were still very much in love. The drive to Springfield was over four hours and we could only see each other four days a month. In most prisons, you can visit every weekend. Our phone calls were much more expensive so we had to limit our calls to three times a week.

It was always wonderful to see Sandy, but in each visit there seemed to always be the same dark cloud hanging over our heads. I could see the pain in her eyes, the feeling of helplessness that wouldn't go away. She told me once that she told God that it was even okay if He made me a preacher, just heal me and send me home.

The books by Norvel Hayes and Kathryn Kuhlman had brought my faith to a feverish pitch. All I talked about was being healed. Sandy and my family thought I was going crazy. Everybody thought I had gone into denial. I wouldn't even consider the fact that I was going to die.

Day after day I had been studying the Bible for hours. I was believing with all my heart and soul that I was going to be healed. My faith was boiling inside of me from the story about Doris's healing in the Kathryn Kuhlman book.

I had learned to bind the disease according to scripture. "Whatever you bind on earth will be bound in heaven" (Matthew 18:18). I had bound the sickness according to God's Word and I knew it could not progress now.

I stood on God's Word in 1 Peter 2:24 that by the stripes of Jesus I was healed. I confessed this hundreds of times daily according to Mark 11:23.

Have you ever shown off for your mom and dad? Did you ever do somersaults as a child and yell out to them until they looked and praised you for your monumental feats? Or bring home a drawing from school that wasn't even intelligible to anyone other than mom and she would put it under a magnet on the refrigerator for everyone to see? And you thought you were the best artist in the world because Mom had put it on the refrigerator. You were willing to risk life and limb for praise from your parents. What they thought about you was the most important thing in the whole world! Well, this is the way I began to think about impressing my Father—my Father in Heaven.

Through reading and understanding the Bible, I had come to a close personal relationship with God. I loved Him and I wanted to show off for Him just like I wanted to show off for Mom and Dad when I was a small child.

One day in March 1995, I was showing off for my Father in Heaven. I was walking the floor in my private one-man cell quoting Scripture and praising the name of the Lord. I knew that I was glorifying God by repeating His words. I was like a small child showing off and asking my Heavenly Father to listen to me.

As I was quoting Scripture, like a bolt of lightning, my faith met my understanding, and I was given a revelation by God. This was where the rubber finally met the road. In a millisecond the Lord revealed to me that I was healed! In a split second the Lord filled my mind and spirit with the gift of faith and healing at the same time.

He told me that His Son, Jesus, my Lord and Savior, had paid the price for all sickness and disease. Jesus willingly gave His life on the cross and through the stripes on His back and His shed blood, the price was paid in full! Healing was mine through the shed blood of Jesus. There was so much more that He told me, but I cannot express it in words. I can only say that "I knew that I knew" that I was healed from that moment on! All praise and all glory be to God forever and ever. Amen!

I was amazed that in the instant the revelation was revealed to me I was able to understand what I had memorized in God's Word. I recalled Luke 10:19: "Behold, I give you the authority to trample on serpents and scorpions, and over all the power of the enemy, and nothing shall by any means hurt you."

The revelation was so powerful I remember saying out loud, "That's it!" And that was it! I was healed. Did I look any different? No. Did I feel any different? No. But that didn't matter because I knew I was healed. I was still thin as a rail, but I was healed and I knew it. Praise God!

I jumped up and down and praised God over and over. I felt an incredible closeness to God. Like He was right there in the room with me. The Holy Spirit of God was indeed there in my little 6 foot x 10 foot prison cell. There are no barriers for God. There is nowhere that His mighty arm can't reach and there is no one that He can't touch.

I couldn't wait to tell Sandy and my family and friends. But when I told them I didn't get the response I thought I would get. I was amazed that they acted so cool to my story. They all said that it was great, but I knew they were just saying that to appease me. I have to admit that I may have responded the same way had I not been the one whom God had spoken to personally. I was hurt, but I accepted the unbelief.

After all, there was no way I could prove it at the time. Or was there? I was sitting on my bunk a few days later and the thought came to my mind to start working out with weights again. Since I had been transferred to Springfield and diagnosed terminal, I was not even allowed to work. And just before I left Terre Haute, I was told that if I was caught even trying to work out that I would be put in the hole. It had now been nine months since I had touched a weight.

But just as soon as the thought came to mind to work out another thought quickly followed: *You better not, Danny. You know how weak your right arm is and if you start working out, you will see how weak your left arm is becoming.* For a split second I froze. Then another thought came, *I thought you were healed.* I thought to myself that I was healed. Then a simple thought said, *Well!* I thought to myself, *What?* Then it came to me. What does a man who is healed do? Anything he wants to do!

That was it! First, I got permission from the doctor to exercise. Then I marched down to the gym. On the way I was flooded with evil thoughts. Thoughts like, *Don't do it or you will probably collapse. Don't go in there or you'll know for sure that you're not really healed after all.* I kept walking and told the devil that he was a liar (John 8:44), that by the stripes of Jesus I was healed (1 Peter 2:24) and that he no longer had any jurisdiction over me because Christ had redeemed me from the curse of the law (Galatians 3:13).

That first day I was incredibly weak, but I was determined to work out anyway. As a matter of fact, I had a very hard time making it back to my cell, but not because I wasn't healed. It was because my cell was so far from the gym and I was already in such a weak state to begin with.

I had a very long road ahead of me to recondition my body and gain back all the muscle mass that I had lost. God had done His part and now it was my turn to do my part through faith that I was healed.

The doctor had been seeing me every other week. Soon after I was healed it was time for another office visit, but I didn't dare mention this to my doctor because I knew he would think I was losing it too. He had diagnosed several patients with Lou Gehrig's and seen them all die.

During the visit he asked me how I was holding up. I simply told him I was trusting in the Lord. He didn't say anything, but he took some notes.

In the first part of April I asked Dr. Klinkerfuss to release me from there and send me back to Terre Haute Camp. After all, I wasn't receiving any treatment (because there was none) and I knew I was healed even though I hadn't said a word to him about it. Besides, why should I have to stay in a prison of walking dead men when I was healed? The doctor told me he wouldn't release me until he personally talked to my judge. He said, "Don't you understand? The only chance you have is to be released so you can get some experimental medication before you die in here."

As I left his office the horrible truth hit me square in the face. They knew that I had Lou Gehrig's before I left Terre Haute Camp! They didn't tell me because they thought I'd run. They thought that anyone with five years left to serve who had been given a death sentence and a prognosis of only a couple of years would more than likely walk away from a camp.

I remembered the doctor had said that he had tested me to try to rule out the diagnosis. But for some reason it hadn't dawned on me until then that he was trying to rule out the diagnosis of Lou Gehrig's that was from the Neurologist at Region Hospital in Terre Haute, Indiana. They had sent me to Springfield to die. They wanted to make sure that I was behind the wall so I couldn't leave. That explained the six-passenger private jet that hustled me out of Indiana so quickly. I was stuck there to die unless the Lord moved on my behalf.

Shortly after the doctor had told me that he wouldn't send me back to a camp, I saw him in the hallway and he told me he decided to call my judge personally. He was put through to the judge's private chambers. He explained in detail the situation to the judge. He told the judge that he would immediately fax his evaluations and diagnosis to the judge for his personal inspection. He told the judge that I had exhausted all of my remedies for release through the Bureau of Prisons, and unless the judge were to do something, I would die in prison without even an opportunity to take the experimental drugs that were available to the general public, but not to me.

The judge said he would consider what the doctor said and in the meantime he wanted my attorney to contact him at the courthouse.

I was beside myself. The Lord had opened another door where there was no door. This was the first time I had been given new hope since the Warden's appeal on my behalf. I told Sandy, but from her point of view it was going to be another bitter disappointment. It was just so hard for her to get her hopes up now after already being turned down three times.

My family decided to retain the very professional law firm of Lewis, Rice & Fingersch in St. Louis, Missouri, for this particular circumstance.

I was to be represented by a man named Barry Short. I had never met my new lawyer, but I was instructed to call him at his office. I called him and he gave me instructions of what to do on my part while he made arrangements to speak with the judge. I was told to compile a history of everything that had happened to me legally and medically since I had been arrested and send it to him so he could familiarize himself with me as quickly as possible.

In the meantime, I learned that the judge had actually written a letter on my behalf directly to the Director of the Bureau of Prisons, Kathleen Hawk. That was incredible. My federal sentencing judge contacted the head of the federal prisons on my behalf.

Shortly after this I saw my Unit Manager in the dining hall and he told me that, in the seventeen years that he had worked in the prison system, he had only seen a federal judge appeal in two other cases and both inmates went home.

He told me not to worry about a transfer back to the camp because I was going home. I thought to myself, *Thanks, Lord. I know I'm going home now.*

About three weeks later, I was told that Kathleen Hawk, the Director of the Bureau of Prisons, had denied the judge's appeal on my behalf. After my fourth straight denial Sandy and my family were destroyed. Still I thanked God for my healing, for my release from prison, and for my wife.

I was only able to hang on by the grace of God. Sandy had come to visit me almost every available visit for the past eight months. Finally, after eight straight months of cruel disappointment she was physically, emotionally, and financially drained. Even though I kept insisting I was healed, she thought I was in denial. I had gained some weight, but not enough to make a noticeable difference.

Sandy came to see me the weekend of my fourth denial to be released from federal prison. We were both strung out. Her hope and faith had been crushed by this latest of many monumental disappointments. We had talked many times of how we would get married the minute I walked out the front door. We had found a wonderful place in Missouri just an hour drive from the prison. It was an old Victorian Style town for persons to get married and spend an old-fashioned honeymoon. There were even horse-drawn carts and moonlight rides. It sounded so romantic. But what now? Our dreams had been shattered once again. I could see the wear and tear in her beautiful blue eyes.

She was still wearing a full dress size smaller than she used to wear, and believe me, she was perfect before. I always called Sandy on Sunday evenings when she left from a visit to make sure she arrived home okay. That night the thing that I feared the most came upon me.

Sandy broke down on the phone. She told me she just couldn't do it anymore. That she would always love me, but she just couldn't visit anymore, she just couldn't. She said that I could call once a week, but that was all and not to expect anything more.

When I hung up the phone I was crushed. I was so afraid to be without her. The thought of doing this without her seemed impossible. I walked slowly back to my cell and when I closed my door I thanked God for my healing, for my release from prison, and for my wife.

I would soon find out that God was still with me no matter what the circumstances looked like. It was in this deepest, darkest valley in my life that I would learn to trust God more than ever before.

Like softened clay on a potter's wheel, I lay on my cell bunk and cried like a baby. I cried to the Lord and said, *Why, Lord. Why does she have to leave me now? I need her more than ever now.*

As torrents of tears covered my pillow, I heard the Lord speak to me in my spirit. He said, *How much do you love her?* I said, *With all my heart, Lord.* He said, *Do you love her enough to not keep any record of the wrong you think she is doing to you right now? Do you love her that much?*

I began to realize that God Himself gave up His only Son for a people who had gone astray. He died for us and He never once complained. He counted it as love. The Lord hadn't asked me to die, He had only asked me to not keep a record of wrongs or rights. Could I do that? In my deepest passion, I grew like I had never grown before and I said. *Yes, Lord, I can love her without question and without keeping a record of the pain I'm feeling right now.* I never heard anything else from the Lord that night, but I felt a peace in a strange way after I surrendered my heart in love.

CHAPTER 17

"I Wish I Had Your Faith"

In the first part of May 1995, I was called to my Unit Manager's Office. He said the staff there was very disappointed that Washington hadn't released me for compassionate reasons. Then he told me that a man dying of cancer had been released from a Federal Prison in Florida two weeks prior on a special appearance bond. He had never seen a bond like this one before and he felt it had set a precedent in that area. He also said that because it was so new it wouldn't even be in the law books yet. He felt I might be able to be released with the same kind of bond. He couldn't allow me to read it, but he gave me the case number and the district where it was filed and the rest was up to me.

By this time my lawyer had talked to the judge and the judge wanted to help, but he said that we must put something in front of him to justify my release. A young lawyer named Stephen Kirsch was put in charge of pulling all the details together in my case for the senior lawyer, Mr. Short. Stephen immediately tracked down all the pertinent information relating to the special bond and began to prepare a motion for compassionate release accompanied by an appearance bond for my release while the judge was considering my motion.

An Appearance Bond was a special bond that would allow me to be released under strict monitoring and house arrest, to go to the Washington University School of Medicine, in St. Louis, Missouri, on

July 20, 1995, at 8:30 A.M. to be considered for the Controlled Experimental Drug Program for Lou Gehrig's victims. This was one of the few experimental programs in progress in the entire country and Washington University is only ten miles from where Sandy lived!

We spent all of May 1995 gathering documented information for the motion to release me and for the Appearance Bond that would allow me to attend the appointment. The screening at Washington University School of Medicine would be the deciding factor as to whether or not the judge ruled in my favor. If I were admitted to the experimental drug program, I would be released from prison and if I wasn't admitted, then the judge would deny my motion.

I had kept in touch with Sandy with weekly calls, but it had been a while since she had visited. I didn't ever push her or try to get her to visit. I only told her that I was there as a friend and I always would be.

The first week of June 1995, the doctor finally said he would transfer me back to Terre Haute Camp. Praise God! Another miracle! I had told the doctor that my attorney assured me it wouldn't make any difference in the judge's ruling whether I was in a camp or a high-level medical penitentiary and it just so happened that Terre Haute Camp was a secondary medical facility anyway.

Before I was to be transferred I needed a haircut. So I went to Ron. Ron was the same man who cut my hair the first time I had it cut when I arrived at Springfield nine months earlier. As Ron was cutting my hair he decided to share something he had kept from me.

Ron told me that before he was arrested, he had often cut the hair of dead men in funeral homes to prepare them to be seen for the last time by their loved ones. He said their hair was always brittle like sticks or straws. He said the first time he cut my hair (nine months prior) it was exactly like the hair of those dead men. He said he knew I was a walking dead man at the time, but he didn't have the heart to say anything to me. But now he told me that my hair was healthy again and he believed I was healed too.

The next week, I was taken to the Federal Transfer Center in Oklahoma City by bus. I was to be held there in transit until I was flown by Conair to the Camp. While I was there, my lawyers overnighted the motion for me to sign so that we could file it in the federal courts. I signed the papers and mailed them immediately back to my lawyers. This was June 26, 1995, only three weeks until the appointment at Washington University School of Medicine.

While I was in Springfield, Sandy had not mentioned visiting me again. She hated Springfield and everything it represented to her. But before I left Springfield she asked me to call her when I got to the Transfer Center. My heart was pounding after the call.

When I called Sandy from Oklahoma City, she was so sweet. For the first time since April she told me she would like to visit me at the camp if I wanted her to. If I wanted her to? Are you kidding me? I wanted to see her more than anything in the world. At this time I hadn't seen her in close to three months. I hadn't mentioned anything about a visit. I knew that it had to be her that made the first move. I was willing to wait patiently no matter how long that took. There was never going to be another Sandy.

I arrived at Terre Haute Prison Camp on June 28th, and three days later I saw Sandy. Would you believe it, it was her birthday? We had been engaged exactly one year, and it had happened right there in the same visiting room. Remember, I hadn't seen Sandy for about three months. When I walked into the visiting room, she was stunned. At Springfield I had to wear those giant baggy jumpsuits during a visit, but at the camp the regulation dress called for green army fatigue pants and a T-shirt. I had been pumping iron for the past three months and eating four big meals a day. I had gained thirty pounds of solid muscle! There was nothing to hide my healing now. What a visit!

It was a bright, sunny July day, and as we walked hand in hand around the visiting room outside area, I could see the sparkle in her sky blue eyes once again. This was the first time I had seen her this happy since I had left the camp ten months earlier.

She wasn't the only one smiling, though. I was smiling because I was with Sandy and I loved her and I was also smiling because I had never stopped trusting God for my healing, my release from prison and to be married to Sandy. Sandy still didn't believe I had a chance to be released, but she did begin to believe I was healed. There were no commitments that weekend, but the fire in our hearts was rekindled just by being together once again.

After our incredible weekend visit, there were only fourteen business days left for the judge to rule. There was nothing to do now but wait and pray.

I was back in Terre Haute Camp. It was so great to be back in a minimum security prison again. The people there were so friendly and I knew most everyone because I had served eighteen months there prior to my ten-month stay in the Springfield Medical Penitentiary. I greeted my old friends and got back to the same Bible studies I was attending before I left. I felt at home there.

It's a very rare circumstance indeed when an inmate wins a motion in court. Almost everyone loses. I remember one day someone was asking me how things were going and I told them I was waiting for the judge to rule on a motion I had before him and it was imperative he rule in the next few days. A man who was standing close enough to hear our conversation said, "Don't get your hopes up, Danny. You know that almost everybody gets shut down." I said, "I know I'm going to win this motion. I'm trusting God for it."

It was a hot July and there was no air-conditioning at the camp. I wasn't assigned a job, so I just walked the track and prayed most of the time in the summer heat. The days went by slowly and many doubts tried to command my attention, but I held fast to my faith and wouldn't let anything or anyone break my spirit.

I had to be in St. Louis at the Washington University School of Medicine at Barnes Hospital at 8.30 A.M. on July 20th and it was now July 5th.

Although Sandy and I had still not made any commitments, she said she would let me stay with her if I were to be released. This was wonderful because if there were any changes at all this close to the ruling, it would hold up everything and a new motion would have to be submitted with the change of information.

Along with the first letter that Sandy sent to my Case Manager in Springfield that confirmed that she would accept responsibility to take care of me, there was also a complete report filed with a Parole Officer in my immediate release area. The Parole Officer scheduled a visit to Sandy's house to confirm that if I were to be released, he had inspected the location that I would be released to and found it satisfactory. If I were to change locations at this late date, the Parole Officer would have to go out and inspect the new location once again to confirm it for the courts. The last time it took two months to do this.

The first week of July passed and not a word. Then the second week was almost over. On Friday, the week before I was to meet my medical appointment, I called my mother. She told me my lawyer had called and if I called her she was to have me call him. Maybe this was it! I would finally know.

I called my lawyer, Stephen Kirsch, and he told me he had gotten so anxious waiting that he called the judge's private chambers to ask what was happening. After all, there would only be three business days left before I had to be released to meet the medical appointment.

He told me he talked to the judge's personal law clerk. The clerk told him the judge had gone on vacation three weeks ago. The judge was on vacation when my motion was filed and he hadn't even seen it yet. The clerk did say that the judge would be back in his chambers on the following Monday. What a shock to both of us. My lawyer was a nervous wreck because he wanted me to win so badly. I told him we still had three more days and that I believed the judge would rule in my favor. He said, "I wish I had your faith."

When Monday came I began to pack my things and get ready to leave. I started giving things away to guys that would help them. I had decided I didn't need to take them home with me. I had a very nice Jewish bunkie at the time and he was amazed that I was packing and I hadn't even heard anything from the courts.

To give away things was unheard of unless you knew for sure you were leaving. Most inmates didn't have much in prison and you were very careful to take very good care of what you did have. This was Monday evening. Remember, I had to be at the hospital by Thursday morning and my family had been told that if I missed my scheduled appointment it would be at least two to three months before I could reschedule. The waiting list was that long.

There was no word all day Tuesday. Finally, it was 4:00 P.M. I knew the business day was over, but there was still one day left. You see, I had to be released the next day now or the Bureau of Prisons wouldn't have enough time to process me out Wednesday and give me enough time to drive 175 miles to St. Louis by 8:30 A.M. Thursday.

At 4:30 P.M. I was standing with a group of inmates talking when the Unit Manager approached us and said, "Where's Cox?" I said, "Right here." He said, "Come with me."

The Unit Manager handed me a small piece of yellow paper with a phone number on it. He said, "Do you know whose number that is?" I said, "Yes, I do." He took me to a telephone and said, "Call it collect from here."

I called and my lawyer answered and before I could even say hello he screamed, "We won the Appearance Bond Motion—You're coming home tomorrow!" Tears welled up in my eyes as my mind soaked up his words. We were both beside ourselves. I had gone through so much and waited so long. My answer was finally there; I was going home the next day! Praise God!

When I went back to the other inmates I told everyone. The word spread like wildfire. Everyone was so excited to see anyone win anything. Most guys came up and congratulated me and shook my hand.

Many thought that I would be dead soon and they were happy that I could get my last days with family.

Mr. Kirsch told me he had already contacted my mother, but Sandy wasn't home so he left a message for her to call him. So I got on the phone to call her and tell her myself.

When I got through to Sandy she had already talked to Kirsch. She was absolutely amazed that I was really going to be released after so many bitter disappointments. It was like the nightmare had turned into a dream now. She told me she had already called her boss and she would pick me up in Terre Haute the next day. My heart almost melted. I was actually going home the next day, after fifty-one months in prison. And I was being taken home by the woman of my dreams.

Sandy and I talked on the phone several times that evening. We were on a cloud. We made lots of little plans and coordinated times. I was going to call her first thing in the morning and give her the last-minute instructions. She had a friend in Terre Haute and she was going to go there and wait for my release time. I had the phone number so I could call her from my Case Manager's Office.

I was called early to turn in my institution property. Then I was told to tell Sandy I would be processed out by 1:00 P.M. Sandy then gave my Case Manager the number she could be contacted at in town and left for the camp.

Just a short distance from the camp was Terre Haute Penitentiary. All important business was first conducted through the Penitentiary. If the business pertained to the camp, then the information was relayed to them.

After Sandy was on her way to her friend's place in the city, I was called down and told there was a problem. When the orders were faxed to the Penitentiary from the courts, not all the documents were there that were needed for my release. They told me that they were in the process of asking the courts to send the documents that they needed, but they weren't sure if they could get them in time and get me out that day.

For a moment my heart sank. Why was there a problem? I was told that they had never seen an Appearance Bond like that before, so they needed more supporting paperwork to confirm the release. Now another waiting game, but I had trusted the Lord this far. Hey! What was a few more hours? I knew that I was going home that day, no matter what the circumstances looked like.

By 1:00 P.M. Sandy was at her friend's apartment. My Case Manager told me to call her and explain the situation and just ask her to stay put. When I called and told Sandy she was very worried about the paperwork. I told her everything would be all right.

Finally, at 3:15 P.M., I was called to control. There was a guard there from the Penitentiary to take me over to the main prison office to finalize my paperwork. He was in a hurry because he said if he didn't get me processed by 4:00 P.M., I would have to stay until the next morning, which would be too late. We rushed and I was back at the camp by 3:40 P.M.. I was told to call my ride. Now Sandy was on her way to pick me up.

The final papers came across the fax machine and we had just a few more details to address. At 3:55 P.M. I could see Sandy walking up the drive. She walked in the control center and walked right up to me and gave me the sweetest hug and kiss. There were a few other inmates in the control center and they were ooohhhing and aaahhhing. At 3:57 P.M. the man from the Penitentiary who was still processing me out and the camp control officer got into an argument about whether or not they could finish the paperwork in time for the four o'clock count (this was the national prison count—the most important of all counts).

The man from the Penitentiary said, "If you don't finish right now, you're going to have to pay me some big overtime." The control officer said, "Okay, okay!" And then he signed the final release papers. At one minute to 4:00 P.M., Sandy and I walked out of the front door of Terre Haute Prison Camp hand in hand on a bright sunny July afternoon.

As we walked down the sidewalk I could hear some of the inmates saying things like, "Good luck" and "God bless you." And still others paid no attention to me, but were whistling at Sandy.

Sandy was stunning that day. She was wearing shorts, a summer top and sandals. This was the first time I had seen her in shorts in four-and-a-half years.

It was hot, at least in the 90's, as we walked toward the car. I could see men lying in their bunks suffocating from the heat. I thought about how many times I was the one watching others leave. It was always someone else, but not that day. I was leaving. After fifty-one months I was leaving. I was still not free yet, because I was released on an Appearance Bond pending the judge's ruling on my motion to vacate the remainder of my sentence, but I was going home that day with the love of my life.

CHAPTER 18

More Tests!

I couldn't wait to get off the prison property. I looked back one more time and then it was out of sight. Thank God! Terre Haute, Indiana, is only seven miles from the Illinois state line. So, in only a matter of minutes we were in the state of Illinois. In two-and-a-half hours I would be at Sandy's house in Collinsville, Illinois.

The trip was very pleasant in Sandy's air-conditioned car. It was great to ride without cuffs and chains. We talked and talked as we drove. It was good to be free, but it still seemed like a dream to me.

I was to report to the U.S. Probation Office bright and early the next morning before my first medical appointment. Sandy took me to the Federal Building in East St. Louis, Illinois, at 8:00 A.M. It was obvious from the very start that being on house arrest wasn't going to be a picnic. I was read a series of strict rules and I had to sign that I understood them and that I would comply with them.

The only places that I was allowed to go was to medical appointments, my lawyer's office and to church, but even these had to be preapproved and I had to call before I left and after I returned from every appointment. Failure to follow these rules would result in an immediate violation of the Appearance Bond. I couldn't go more than 100 feet from the house when I was there and I had to be available to answer a phone call from my probation officer any time of the day or night. But even with all these rules and restrictions, I was thankful to be home. I'd been under strict authority for years now anyway.

We left the probation office and Sandy took me to the Washington University School of Medicine. I went to the Division of Neurology and checked in. I got a seat in the waiting room and settled in.

After a short while, I was ushered to a small examining room. I was then examined by a neurologist and then by another neurologist. They were completely aware of my circumstances and they told me they were going to set some medical appointments so that they could run a series of tests on me. I would have to go through the same tests I had already been through, plus even more now.

My mother picked me up because Sandy had gone on to work and I went straight home. I was amazed at all the people who were going in every direction in Barnes Hospital. I had forgotten what a rat race the world really was.

I had always thought that as soon as I was released, I'd be able to adjust back to a normal life in nothing flat. After all, what would be hard about just being myself?

It didn't take me long to realize that I had been told what to do and when to do it for so long I had all but lost the ability to make decisions, even small ones. I remember that at one of our first meals Sandy asked me if I wanted to drink milk, juice, soda, or water for dinner. I actually couldn't make up my mind. It had been years since I had that many choices at once. Finally, I asked her to cut it down to two choices and I'd choose one.

I had been browbeat and treated like a loser for so long that my self-esteem was at an all-time low. I was calling everybody "Sir" and

"Ma'am," and acting like I was still under some invisible authority. I do remember that on one of the first nights at Sandy's, something happened that made me feel very good. Sandy's bedroom was at one end of the house and her son, Blake, was in his bedroom at the other end of the house. I was sleeping on the couch in the living room in the middle of the house, between the two.

Just after we had all gone to bed, Blake yelled out to Sandy and said, "Mom, did you remember to set the alarm? I'm scared." Sandy said, "Blake, you know that Danny is on the couch right by the front door, so don't worry." Blake said, "That's right! Good night, Mom. Good night, Danny." For the first time in a very long time, I felt like someone really needed me. Like my presence made a difference, even if it was only to make a little boy feel safe.

My first two weeks at Sandy's were indeed rocky. Even though Sandy loved me and said she couldn't wait to get me home, she seemed to have a hard time adjusting to my presence. She and Blake had lived alone for so long that it was hard for her to adjust to me too.

I also felt funny because nothing was mine. I had always owned everything I needed, but now I had nothing of my own. I was impulsive and I tried to overcompensate in many areas such as the dinner table. I had a tendency to start cleaning up before everyone was even finished eating. And I would wash the dishes during the day and put them away where I thought they should go. When Sandy came home to fix dinner, she couldn't find anything.

The list goes on and on, but by the end of my second week at Sandy's, we both felt very uncomfortable. Then it happened. Sandy came home on a Friday after work and said, "We have to talk." I knew this was going to be serious. She told me she felt that things just weren't working between us. As much as I hated to admit it, she was right. I didn't feel right either. I just didn't feel like I belonged there.

We both expressed our concerns about each other and agreed that I would call the probation officer first thing Monday morning and ask him if I could relocate to my mother's house. It was already too late on Friday, so I would have to spend the weekend. That was fine with Sandy. She didn't want to stop seeing me. She just felt she needed time to adjust to the circumstances.

As strange as it sounds, we both felt better once we agreed I would move to my mother's. We could work out our relationship from there. We both still loved each other, but we just couldn't live together under all the pressure on our relationship.

As the evening wore on, we joked and laughed and had a wonderful time. The pressure was finally off. I felt like a new man. I loosened up and started being relaxed for a change. As soon as I did, the entire atmosphere seemed to change. It was light and lively and so much fun to be with Sandy. I could see it in her mood too. She now had a choice, an option that she previously didn't have.

That weekend, in the space of two days, our whole lives changed. We were like high school sweethearts again. When Monday morning came we were having coffee before Sandy went to work. Neither of us addressed the agreement of me talking to my probation officer, but I was going to make the call after she went to work.

I walked her to the door and gave her a kiss good-bye for the day and after she kissed me, she said, "Why don't you wait a couple of days before you call the probation officer?" My heart almost jumped out of my chest, but I casually said, "Okay." But after she left I went into the spare bedroom and lay on the floor with tears in my eyes and thanked the Lord.

After that weekend everything changed. We began to fall in love all over again. We couldn't wait to see each other when Sandy got home from work and she couldn't wait to see me when I got back from the medical appointments. Our love was igniting like a forest fire.

I was scheduled for test after test. The doctors were compiling a file on me. The judge would rule whether or not to release me from prison after the chief neurologist made his final diagnosis and prognosis.

Sandy and I fell so deeply in love that I thought she might want to marry me now. So I asked my mother to get me two gold wedding bands.

One evening I asked Sandy to sit on the edge of her bed for a minute. When she did I got on my knees in front of her and asked her if she wanted to marry me. I told her I was not asking to set a date. I just wanted to know if she still would like to marry me. She said, "Yes, I do." I pulled out the gold bands and put one on her finger and she put one on mine. She said, "I'll never take this ring off, ever." I was so proud.

A few days later she asked me one night if I thought the pastor at a local church could marry us the next day. I had taken the liberty to get the marriage license (just in case) while she was at work. My heart was pounding like a bass drum as I talked to the pastor on the phone. He said we could come by the church at 10:15 A.M. the next morning and he could marry us in a private ceremony in the chapel.

We were there right on time. We were both scared, not knowing what the future would bring, but knowing we wanted to live our lives together for the rest of our lives. Nothing could stop how we felt about each other.

We were married in church by a pastor and I thanked God for giving me Sandy to be my lawfully wedded wife.

After being home for thirty days, the chief neurologist made his diagnosis. He said that I did not have Lou Gehrig's disease. Praise God! Then he sent his report to the judge.

On August 23, 1995 (thirty-four days after I had been released on bond), I got a call from the probation officer. He told me to be in his office that day by 2:00 P.M. When I got there he took a snapshot of me and stapled it to an order to report back to Terre Haute Federal Prison Camp by 2:00 P.M. the next day. I was ordered to go back to prison and serve out the remainder of my ten-year sentence. I felt like I had been stabbed in the back with a knife.

Sandy and I spent a quiet evening together alone and as close as we could because we knew that the morning would come soon enough, and it did.

It was a long drive back to Terre Haute Prison Camp. When I got there, the walk from the parking lot to the front door was the longest, hardest walk I had ever made. It was even harder than facing my original ten-year sentence. This time I had to leave a family that I loved with all my heart.

I would have to serve another four-and-a-half years before I could be with my family again. The pain was almost too much to bear. I had just left this place thirty-five days earlier, and now, on another scorching summer day in August 1995, I self-surrendered to serve the balance of my ten-year prison sentence. The government added the thirty-five days that I was out on bond back onto the remaining sentence.

Sandy walked into the control center with me while I checked in. I could see the tears begin to well in her blue eyes, so I said, "You better go, Honey. I don't want you to see them take me into custody." We kissed one last kiss and she walked back down the sidewalk to the parking lot, except this time she was without me!

I talked to Sandy later that night and she said the house was so empty without me. She had grown to love coming home to me, the sound of my voice in the house, and the clump clump of my big feet on the hardwood floors. Sandy's house was now our house, but I wasn't there to share it with her. She told me it just wasn't the same anymore without me. She missed me terribly and she cried on the phone. I knew before I was released on bond that I would probably lose my motion to be released, but no matter what, you can't be prepared to return to prison. I was numb the first few days. I didn't feel like I belonged there anymore. I had finally adjusted to being at home and now I was having a hard time adjusting to prison life again. All I talked about were Sandy and Blake. I know this was hard on the other men who were lonely and homesick too.

About three weeks after I returned to the camp, I had a very shocking phone conversation with Sandy. She told me she was late for her monthly period. I told her she must be stressed out from all the traumatic things that had happened in our lives recently. She said she had been late now for three weeks and that just wasn't like her in any circumstances.

After another week Sandy was so concerned that she bought a pregnancy test kit. When I called that night she told me that the test is blue when you're not pregnant and it moves from pink to red when you are pregnant. She told me that she had just taken the test and it went straight to red! "I'm pregnant," she said. Pregnant? How could this be? We had been very cautious. We had talked about more children when I was home, but we had agreed that since we already had Blake, and I already had Stephanie, we wouldn't have any more children. When I was first diagnosed terminal we thought that I would be released very soon, so we made plans to marry as soon as I was released. Sandy had also gone to the doctor immediately and gotten a prescription for birth control pills. Finally, after I had been turned down four times in a row for a compassionate release, she decided to stop taking the pill. She stopped taking the pill in May 1995, and I was released in July 1995. She had taken the pill for eight months and then only two months before I was released she stopped taking the pill because she had given up hope that I would be released. And now we were expecting a baby! What a surprise!

Something that I had not prayed for happened. I had prayed for my healing and received it. I had prayed for a perfect mate and I got one. I had prayed to be released from prison and I had been. But now the Lord had moved in our lives in an unexpected way. I sought the Bible for an answer and I found it very quickly in Psalm 127:3-5:

> Behold, children are a heritage of the LORD,
> The fruit of the womb is His reward.
> Like arrows in the hand of a warrior,
> So are the children of one's youth.
> Happy is the man who has his quiver full of them.

Praise God!

CHAPTER 19

It's a Brother

When I was in Springfield, I talked to Sandy continually about us having a baby, but when I went home for thirty-five days, we decided not to have any more children. Now we were going to have a baby for sure.

The next few weeks were the most difficult. Sandy's chemical balance was changing daily and the thought of having a baby without me was weighing heavily on her mind. She was very moody and there was nothing I could do to cheer her up. She even threatened to divorce me. But, after the first three months, she stabilized and we began to talk about how wonderful it was going to be to have a baby. Sandy had an ultrasound test to see if the baby was a girl or boy. The doctor was unavailable that day so the nurse conducted the test. After a considerable amount of time, the nurse declared that she couldn't detect the male private parts, so the baby must be a girl.

She told me all about the ultrasound that night on the phone, so from that day forward, we started looking for the perfect name for our daughter. As many of you well know, that is a major project.

Sandy was always so concerned that she was getting fat and ugly and I was always so proud of how beautiful she was during pregnancy. On the days that she felt well we had wonderful visits. There is a certain lovely spirit that the Lord gives to a woman during pregnancy. My wife was the perfect example of how beautiful a woman becomes during that time.

During Christmas Sandy was approaching her fifth month. She came to see me over the Christmas holidays and we took a picture on Santa's lap in the visiting room so we would always be able to show our baby how much in love we were and how happy we were that a baby was on the way. We were also given stockings full of Christmas goodies that Sandy took home for Blake. The next day, after our pictures on Santa's lap, a man came in the visiting room for a visit with his family. Sandy said that the man looked really mean and spooky. She asked who he was. I told her that she ought to know because she was sitting on his lap yesterday. It was our inmate, Santa!

Shortly after Christmas, Sandy began a project to decorate the spare bedroom to get it ready for the baby. Her sister Chris was an angel and painted the room so Sandy wouldn't have to inhale the paint fumes. She had also picked out some cute wallpaper to trim the wall. Everything she bought was pink and yellow.

At this time Sandy was seeing the doctor once a month for the checkups. In February (almost seven months), she decided to talk to the doctor about decorating and buying new clothes for the baby. She told the doctor that she was buying everything for a girl and he had better be right because it was so much work getting everything in order.

The doctor said, "Well, maybe we ought to take one more ultrasound test just in case. Okay?" The doctor started the test and shortly afterwards he said, "There's his thing. He is definitely a boy!" Sandy couldn't believe it. I had even told her the first test may not be correct considering how early in the pregnancy it was taken, but she insisted until then. Either way we were both overjoyed that our baby was perfect according to the image on the ultrasound screen.

Now Sandy had to make several trips back to the stores to return all the girl clothes she had purchased and start looking for new wallpaper for a boy, not to mention that we had to start all over trying to find a suitable name for our son. We still had a few months left so Sandy got another book and started giving me the names she liked to see what I thought.

As the time got closer I wanted to be there for the baby's birth so bad. It was going to be such a special time and I didn't want to miss out. I came up with a great idea. I'd ask for an emergency furlough with a prison guard escort.

I knew that if it were approved, I would have to provide the wages of the officer that would accompany me for the day. But since it was only a two-and-a-half hour drive each way, the cost per hour would be within our reach.

I filled out an inmate request to staff and waited for an answer. It didn't take long for the staff to reject the request, saying that childbirth didn't constitute an emergency.

We were very, very disappointed. Then we came up with the next best plan. Sandy got the phone number of the obstetrics ward that she would be in immediately after childbirth. I put the number on my approved calling list a month in advance. Each expectant mother was allowed to have one person with her in the delivery room. Since I couldn't be there, her sister Chris offered to stand in for me. Sandy and Chris are very close.

Chris was going to do two very important things. One, she would set up a camera on a tripod to video the birth. Second, she would take a camera and take as many pictures as possible. Next, she would rush out to a one-hour film developing service and have the pictures developed immediately and put them in the mail, next day delivery.

Since Sandy was going to have a Caesarean birth, we knew in advance the exact time of the birth. Our son would be born on May 6, 1996.

On the morning of Monday, May 6, I was locked down for a count in my cell until 8:25 A.M. As soon as the count was cleared, I headed straight for a phone and called the hospital.

I remember a nurse answering the phone. I asked if she could tell me how Sandy Cox was. She asked me to hold. Then I heard the sweetest little voice say, "Hi, Honey." It was Sandy! She was in the recovery room and they handed the phone right to her. I was amazed. She told me we had a beautiful 7 lb. baby boy with golden hair. I was so happy that tears were running down my cheeks as we talked. I had been praying for Sandy and the baby since I had heard of his conception. I was trusting God that he would be perfect in every way and he was.

That day, May 6, 1996, Garrett Daniel Cox was born into our family. It was one of the happiest days of our lives.

I couldn't wait for the mail call the next day. Sure enough, the overnight package with fifty pictures of Sandy and Garrett arrived right on time. Just thirty-two hours after his birth, I was able to see Garrett. What a blessing! Of course, as the proud father, I showed everyone who would look.

One of the neatest pictures of all was a picture of Blake cradling Garrett in his arms just an hour after his birth. It was such a heartwarming picture. Sandy told me that Blake had gone to the gift shop while she was having Garrett and got some cigars (made of gum) that said—IT'S A BROTHER—and was passing them out. What a wonderful thing for a brother to do! My heart swelled with pride!

Garrett was born on May 6th and my birthday is on May 17th. Sandy wanted to come to see me on my birthday and bring Garrett if she was able. Her sister, Chris, had again offered to help. Chris wasn't on my visiting list at the time, so Chris would come with Sandy and carry Garrett to the door for her, and then wait in town in a motel room until our visit was over. Then she would pick Sandy up at the door and again carry Garrett back to the car for us.

I had already made arrangements with the staff for Sandy to use a private staff restroom to nurse Garrett that was outside of the visiting room. This was a blessing because she would have to feed him several times during a visit.

Sandy told me on a Thursday night that she would be there the next day on my birthday with Garrett. I was ecstatic all day on Friday waiting for visiting hours to begin.

Sandy had to carry Garrett about forty feet from the control center to the visiting room in his car seat, but this was no problem. Finally, I heard my name called for a visit.

Sandy was just inside the visiting room lobby and Garrett was fast asleep in his car seat on the floor right beside her. First, I hugged and kissed the woman I loved with all my heart, then I reached down and picked up my son, Garrett Cox, eleven days old.

I felt like the only father in the whole world. I fought back the tears of joy as we went into the visiting room and found seats. I took Garrett out of his car seat with Sandy giving me careful instructions to watch that I supported his head properly and held him. Just eleven days after his birth, on my birthday, I was holding a perfect gift from God in my arms.

I was smiling from ear to ear while I was holding my son. You couldn't have found a prouder father than me. He was part Sandy and part me, but all Garrett.

Each child is part of their mother and father, but uniquely made by the hand of God.

Psalm 139:13-16:

> For You have formed my inward parts;
> You have covered me in my mother's womb.
> I will praise You, for I am fearfully and wonderfully made;
> Marvelous are Your works
> And that my soul knows very well.
> My frame was not hidden from You,
> When I was made in secret,
> And skillfully wrought in the lowest parts of the earth.
> Your eyes saw my substance, being yet unformed.
> And in Your book they all were written
> The days fashioned for me,
> When as yet there were none of them.

That visit was incredible. And all the visits after that were great. I tried to be the perfect father when Garrett came. I changed his diapers and fed him and held him. I wasn't allowed to be a part of my daughter's life when she was a baby so I wanted to be a part of all that I could with my son.

The trips were still a two-and-a-half-hour drive to Terre Haute Camp. I was aware that there was another medium-security prison and prison camp that had been built in Greenville, Illinois, just thirty-five miles from where we lived. My next move was to ask to be transferred to Greenville so Sandy and the boys would only have a forty-five-minute drive to visit. This way they could visit one day at a time and go home that night. It would be so convenient and inexpensive to visit and I could see them every weekend.

I put in a request to be transferred to Greenville, Illinois, Prison Camp. I was promptly denied for medical reasons. I was able to secure a release from the Chief Medical Officer and I presented it to staff. I was then denied for several other reasons that I felt were inappropriate. I tried again and was denied again. The Bureau of Prisons policy is that an inmate is to be in the appropriate security level institution that is closest to his/her release location. Greenville was thirty-five miles from home and Terre Haute was 165 miles from home. At this time I had already served over five years with perfect conduct in locations that were far from home and so hard on my family and friends.

I put together all the pertinent information as to why I felt that I had been denied a transfer for inappropriate reasons and sent it my mother. My mother then contacted the office of U.S. Representative for Illinois, Jerry Costello. His office was very responsive and immediately began to investigate the situation on behalf of my wife, my children, and our extended families. I can't say enough about the respect and professional help that was rendered on our behalf from Mr. Costello's office.

I had been denied a transfer twice in June 1996, but on July 17, 1996, I walked in the front door of Greenville Illinois Federal Prison

Camp totally due to the monumental effort put forth by Congressman Jerry Costello and his efficient staff of professionals. I thanked God for His goodness.

There is a group of Christian inmates in Greenville Camp called the Prayer Warriors. As soon as I was assigned to a unit, I was met by one of the Prayer Warriors named Kevin Cole. He showed me around and gave me a bag of things like soap, shampoo, and shower shoes to get me by until my property followed me from Terre Haute Prison Camp.

The Prayer Warriors had a mutual fund that they contributed to as a tithing ministry, to help all inmates new to the institution. They freely gave the things that would help new inmates settle in as easily as possible. It was a real blessing to all new arrivals.

They invited me to join them in a designated room after the 9 o'clock count for prayer. The Prayer Warriors met every night to pray for family, friends, and anyone who was brought before the group.

Greenville Prison had just opened in November 1994. Many inmates from Terre Haute Camp had been transferred there at the time. I had been approved to transfer with them, but I was flown to Springfield Medical Prison in September that same year. When I got back to Terre Haute Camp ten months later, those inmates were already in Greenville.

When some of the men from Terre Haute went to Greenville, they joined the Prayer Warriors. One of the first things they did was to hold me up in prayer nightly because they had heard of my diagnosis. And now, here I was. The same guy that most of them had never seen, but had prayed for months on end.

Even though this camp was only 100 miles from Terre Haute Prison Camp it took me two weeks to get there. You figure it out. I didn't attend the first night because I was exhausted from the trip in chains, but I joined the Prayer Warriors my second night and never missed again.

As Kevin Cole and I became very close friends, he asked me to give my testimony for a Wednesday night Bible study. I had never really given my testimony before. I told him I would, but I needed a little time to prepare.

There were only about 195 inmates in this camp and the normal attendance for the Wednesday night Bible study had been about eight to twelve men. On the night of my testimony, the small chapel was packed with about forty men. They said this was the biggest crowd that had ever attended the Wednesday night study.

Many men were intrigued with the mystery of how I could have a wife and baby two months old when I had been incarcerated over five years already. Greenville was a small Prison Camp and the visiting room was even smaller. Many had seen my wife and son there several times. I told them that if they wanted to find out how I had come to have a baby after being incarcerated for more than five years, they would have to come and hear the story in person. Others wanted to hear how I lived after being struck with the ruthless Lou Gehrig's disease.

I had written down pages of notes. There was so much to tell. As I gave my testimony, there was silence in the room. I watched the faces of the men as I told my incredible story. Many times we have a tendency to judge the work that God is doing through us by the emotions we can see and not by what is happening in their heart. Remember, inmates are conditioned to act tough. Crying in public is something they usually avoid at all costs.

As I finished telling about the miracles that God had performed in my life, I told them I appreciated their coming. Still, you could hear a pin drop.

For a moment I thought no one was even affected by my testimony, then the whole room stood and clapped. Men came up and hugged me and told me that my testimony was one of the most powerful stories they had ever heard. Others, with watery eyes, and still others, told me it was all they could do to keep from crying.

Then one man said, "So you're the Danny Cox we've been praying about for the past two years." I said, "Yes, I am." Believe me, God was with me. All I had to do was be faithful to tell the story and He would do the work in the hearts of the men.

Shortly after this, I was asked to be the Chapel Clerk, another blessing from God. In this job I had many duties for the religious disciplines, but typing was a main duty. I typed pages and pages of material for the chaplain.

He also told me I could type anything that pertained to spiritual work. After this I began to feel the push of the Lord to write out my testimony. He had provided the perfect setting and I had been given permission from my boss. So I set out to give an account of the miracles God had manifested in my life in a short twenty-page booklet.

Next, I was approached by the Prayer Warriors again to give my testimony a second time. Many of the men who had heard my testimony in the Wednesday night Bible Study were so touched that they wanted their families to hear the testimony too.

At Greenville Camp our visitors were allowed to attend church with us when they visited on Sundays. And once a month the chaplain let an inmate give the sermon. They wanted me to give my testimony the next available time an inmate could speak. I told them I would discuss it with my wife. Even though the final decision would be mine, I respected my wife's opinion and wishes very much.

I talked to Sandy and she said I had her blessing to give my testimony before the church. She also invited her sister Chris to come with her that day too.

Many men had asked for special visiting privileges for that day to get more of their family approved to visit. Our normal church attendance was about fifty, but that day was the biggest crowd they ever had, except on Father's Day. Every seat was filled and more brought in.

I was scared. I had never addressed that many people before. Nonetheless, I knew I had to give glory to God for the many miracles He had worked in our lives.

As I stood behind the podium, I looked out over what seemed to be a great multitude to me and my eyes drifted to my wife and son who was sitting on her lap. She was sitting in the front row with her sister, Chris, and her two-year-old daughter, Hanna. I was scared, but no man could have been more proud standing before his wife and son as I was giving my testimony. Garrett was just three months old, but he sat quietly looking around as I told of the goodness of God.

There were many women and children this time. I saw wet eyes everywhere as the story unfolded. It took forty-five minutes to tell about miracles that God had performed in my life, and when I was finished, many hearts were touched.

After church was over, we had to go back to the visiting room. There I was approached by person after person to tell me how the story had touched them. Once again, God had done His work in their hearts.

Later that night, at the Prayer Warriors meeting, I heard testimony after testimony from the Prayer Warriors about how my testimony had blessed them again. I had expressed my concerns that those who had already heard my testimony would be bored a second time.

One man said that even though he had been present for the first testimony and knew the whole story, he was on the edge of his seat throughout the testimony waiting to hear every detail again.

God had given me the confirmation that I needed to know that He would bless the testimony if I would just be faithful to give it. Only God's anointing has the power to touch lives and as long as His anointing rests on my testimony, hearts will always be touched.

While at Greenville Prison Camp, I was informed that I would have to be transferred one more time before my release. I was going to be moved to Yankton, South Dakota. But before I left I was allowed to stay in Greenville Camp for eleven months. In that time I saw Sandy, Blake, and Garrett often. I saw Sandy and Garrett almost every weekend for the whole time I was there.

I got to watch Garrett grow every time I saw him. We played with him every visit and I continued to be as much of a father as the circumstances permitted. I really enjoyed taking my family to church too.

One particular Sunday when I was scheduled to read scripture in front of the church congregation, Blake asked if he could stand by me while I read. He was ten years old at the time. I was honored that he would ask and I read while he stood close at my side.

Before I was to leave for Yankton Camp, I was able to see Garrett do something very special. I had seen him crawl in the visiting room, but I had never seen him walk Sandy told me he had been getting bolder and bolder, but most boys don't walk until they are about a year old and Garrett had just turned eleven months.

One morning, as soon as the visiting room was open, I was called for a visit. It was about 8:15 A.M. and there were only a few people in the visiting room at this time. I arrived in the visiting room before Sandy, and I was waiting for her to come in from the lobby. She was holding Garrett in her arms when she walked in, but before I could walk over to her she said, "Stop right there. I want to show you something. Get on your knees and call him." I got on my knees and said, "Garrett! Garrett! Come to Daddy. Come to Daddy." Sandy stood him up right beside her and I continued to call him. Finally, he started to slowly wobble toward me. Step after wobbly step until he fell in my arms.

I saw him walk for my first time and what a blessing. All the people right behind us started clapping. It was so quiet that I had gotten everyone's attention when I was calling Garrett. They were happy for him too, so they clapped for him. That was his first ovation.

Sandy didn't bring the kids every visit. We made time to visit alone together too. We called it our date nights. We spent many hours talking and falling in love over and over. We were still like high school sweethearts.

Then the time finally came. I had to move again. On June 13, 1997, I was transferred to Yankton, South Dakota, Federal Prison Camp. I was in transit for two weeks and I arrived in South Dakota June 27, 1997.

One year after I arrived, I again felt a push from the Lord. This time it was to write this book—to tell in detail about all the wonderful things the Lord has done for me and my family.

Many times God has brought miracles into my life while in prison and He has not finished yet. I was able to meet a prisoner named Bob Darrah. Bob's continual prodding and words of encouragement have caused the writing of this book. He is from the Yankton area so his wife lives not too far away. He offered (he offered his wife) to help in any way they could for Sandy and the kids to visit. Bob's wife, Saundra, is a sweetheart and offered to pick up Sandy at the airport and drive her and the kids to Yankton to a motel. They all visit for the weekend and then Saundra drives Sandy back to the airport after visiting is over on Sunday. What a blessing!

But even with all of Saundra's help, it is extremely difficult for Sandy to visit. Sandy has to take off work early on a Friday, get someone to take her to the airport and arrange to be picked up. Many times the plane has been late and Sandy has to wait for hours in the airport with impatient children, not to mention when the plane is late going back after the visit with two worn-out kids.

Unless Sandy were to write this part herself (she has graciously declined), you will never get the real picture of how much sacrifice is involved in being a good mother and wife with a husband in prison. I can only make a feeble attempt to express how hard it really is for her and the kids. Once she even told me that it was so difficult waiting for me that she hoped she would never hold it against me when I came home. I thank God that she has been able to bear up under the extremely difficult path she has chosen to take to be my wife. I pray that she will continue to keep her eyes on the Lord for He is her source of strength.

I have also had the privilege to meet a young man named Bill Gerard. Bill has graciously read, critiqued and edited the first writing of this book to help it be much better than the original. Thanks, Bill.

As I write this book I have now been in Yankton, South Dakota, Federal Prison Camp for almost fifteen months and in prison for seven-and-a-half years.

CHAPTER 20

Are You High on a Lie?

Each day we face many decisions. God has given us a free will to choose to do right or to do wrong, but God's perpetual law of sowing and reaping cannot be broken. Every action provokes a like action, good producing good and bad producing bad. Galatians 6:7-9 says:

> "Do not deceive yourselves; no one makes a fool of God. You will reap exactly what you plant. If you plant in the field of your natural desires, from it you will gather the harvest of death; if you plant in the field of the Spirit, from the Spirit you will gather the harvest of eternal life. So let us not become tired of doing good; for if we do not give up, the time will come when we will reap the harvest."[6]

As a small child, I was exposed to alcoholism and violence. Then, after my father was killed in a car wreck, I was raised in a single parent family unit by my mother and grandmother. I didn't have a father there to guide and discipline me in godly love. I didn't understand how a man and woman were supposed to live together in marriage. I'm sure this type of upbringing had something to do with my relationship with

---

[6] *Good News Bible, Today's English Version*, Second Ed. (Nashville, TN: Thomas Nelson Publishers, 1992), 240.

women and the way I began to separate myself from the idea of marriage from an early age.

But, even in the worst scenarios, God has His way of working in our lives behind the scenes. Soon after my father was killed, I went to City Temple Church and got saved. I was then baptized in the Mississippi River in an old-time prayer meeting. The Lord opened the doors for the little poor kid from the projects to come to Him and I did. But soon after that, I chose to run from Him. God won't always chase you down and drag you back to Him. No, He'll let you run as hard as you can until you get to the end of your chain and then you'll stop yourself dead in your own tracks.

Even at twelve years of age, I knew the love of the Lord was sweet, but I allowed the world and all its promises and forbidden fruit to take me captive. Leading a life of sin through pleasure doesn't set you free. It enslaves you. It owns you, but you're taken captive very slowly so you're not aware that you're captive until the chains of your captivity are so strong that you can't break free. Then, for many, it's too late!

And even though I was still running from the Lord when I opened my first business, He blessed the work of my hands. I was successful in everything I touched. I prospered financially. I was allowed to improve my God-given talents in the business world even though I'm sure God had different plans for me than owning and operating a nightclub, among my other businesses.

But then I went too far. I started dabbling with drugs and that was the beginning of the end. It was only a matter of time until my own free will brought my life down in flames.

After sowing bad seeds for years, I finally received a harvest equal to my deeds. At forty-two I was arrested on drug charges and sentenced to ten years in federal prison.

It was then and only then that I was ready to receive the truth back into my life. It was only then that I was ready to stop believing the lie straight from hell that I had come to believe as reality. I had been deceived for so long that many things that I thought were right were totally wrong. I was high on Satan's lies!

I was still single and had never been married when I was arrested. I had even bragged that "variety was the spice of life," when in reality, this is contrary to God's Word. It took a lot of time reading God's Word for me to change my way of thinking so I could get in line with His Word. Only when you're in line with God's Word will you begin to be blessed by God.

I thank God that He came to me only one week after I was in jail and wooed me back to Him. From that day forward my life has been changed and I'm still growing in a godly way. The minute I decided to follow Jesus for the rest of my life, He began to lift the veil of deception away from my eyes so I could see the truth.

You'll never know the real truth until you begin to read the Word of God and let it sink into your spirit. John 8:32 says, "And you shall know the truth, and the truth shall make you free." As I began to know the truth, I was set free, even though I was still behind bars.

You don't have to be behind bars to be in prison. I was more in prison while I was free than I am now. I have seen people who have huge incomes and big homes who are constantly depressed and unhappy. Money will not necessarily make you happy. You can have money and be happy, but, in and of itself, money alone can't make you happy. I know because I've been there. The only true happiness and peace are with God. There are many temporary thrills and a lot of false security, but there is absolutely no true happiness without God.

If you're trying to convince yourself, as you read, that you're truly happy and you don't have a personal relationship with Jesus Christ, you're simply fooling yourself. You are deceived with the glitter, pleasure and false security that this world has to offer.

Once I developed a personal relationship with Jesus Christ, He didn't just open the prison doors and set me free. No, I have had to pay for the wrong decisions I have made. Anyone who continues to make bad decisions will also have to pay for them at some time. But once you're a child of God, He begins to work in your life to turn the curses that you have brought upon yourself into blessings. Oh, it won't always be apparent at first, but if you'll trust in the Lord with all of your heart and lean not to your own understanding (Proverbs 3:5), He will begin to do things in your life that are truly miracles.

As I write this book, I'm still in prison. I was arrested on April 10, 1991, and I have already served seven-and-a-half years in prison. I will have served over eight years by the time I am released.

During the past seven-and-a-half years in prison, I have served time in six different county and city jails and twelve federal prisons. Fourteen months of this time were served in county jails including nine months in St. Clair County Jail (Gladiator School). In all, I have served time in eighteen correctional facilities.

In all this time, through penitentiaries to prison camps, the Lord has not allowed me to be harmed, even though many times I have been in harm's way.

As I look back over the places and events that have taken place that I didn't understand at the time, I realize God was teaching me something everywhere that I've been. Even in the dregs of prison, there is a ministry of love and service, and if you're open to it and willing to serve God no matter where you are, He has a ministry for you.

God is continually providing fertile ground for me to sow new seeds of love and humbleness. My heart was changed forever in one day in the St. Clair County Jail. I'm now willing to let the Lord use me to help others for His glory and my personal victory.

I have loved and followed the Lord faithfully for over seven years now and I'm only sorry that I spent so many years in darkness thinking that I had it "going on." I thought I knew it all, but I knew nothing. I was living a life straight from hell. God, in His gracious love, waited for me for thirty years with His arms open wide. He didn't browbeat me like the penal system for my wrongdoing. He has simply forgiven me and asked me to change and be like His Son, Jesus Christ.

This book has been written to witness the miracles that God has manifested in my life. My daughter, Stephanie, is close to her degree at Southern Illinois University and doing well. God has cured me from an incurable disease. He released me from prison for thirty-five days right in the middle of a ten-year prison sentence. During the thirty-five days that I was on house arrest, God gave me a wife, a family and a home. Nine months later He gave us a beautiful baby boy.

It has been over three years since Sandy and I have been married and she is even more beautiful today than she was then. My stepson, Blake, is now eleven years old and he is very athletic. He has a bright future ahead of him. My son, Garrett, is two years old. I was able to see him about two months ago and for the first time he called me "Da-Dee," the word that a father lives to hear!

Remember, I'm just an average person. You're just as precious to God as I am. He isn't a respecter of persons. If He healed me, He can heal you too, or provide you with whatever miracle you desperately need in your life.

Have you ever once been close to God, but right now you're turned away from Him like I was for so many dark years? Or, are you one who has never experienced the only true peace and miracle-working power in your life that only God Himself can give?

I believe that this very day God has used me as an instrument, through this book, to draw you to Him. It's no accident that you're reading this book because God loves you so very much.

Over seven years ago, in the county jail, someone wrote to me and sent some scriptures to me from the Bible that changed my life forever. Today, the Lord has given me the following verses for you:

"That if you confess with your mouth the Lord Jesus and believe in your heart that God has raised Him from the dead, you will be saved. For with the heart one believes unto righteousness, and with the mouth confession is made unto salvation... For 'whoever calls upon the name of the LORD shall be saved'" (Romans 10:9-10,13).

Just two days ago a man died here in prison. I heard him say just a few weeks ago that he was working hard to get in good shape before his birthday. He was running and jogging daily and appeared to be in good shape.

He turned fifty on Wednesday and he died in his sleep on Thursday. He was to be released the very next day on Friday. The Bible says that no one knows the day, hour, or minute that we will die. But the Apostle Paul makes it clear in Hebrews 9:27 that *all* men (and women) are appointed to die once, then we will be judged!

This man didn't know that when he went to sleep on Wednesday he would never wake up on Thursday. Can any one of us be sure that we will wake up from any night's sleep? There is only one way to escape judgment for our sins and that is through the Son of God.

Where do you stand this day? If you were to go to bed tonight and not wake up tomorrow, would you be saved? Would you go to heaven? If you are not absolutely positive, then you need to make the most important decision you have ever made right now—a decision to make Jesus the Lord and Savior of your life.

Jesus shed His innocent blood and died on the cross for our sins. There is no way that any one of us can ever pay for our own sins. If we die without having our sins blotted out through the blood of Jesus, we will be judged by our every action at the White Throne Judgment. Those who have asked the only Son of God for forgiveness and asked Him to cleanse us from our unrighteousness will be saved through the blood of Jesus.

If you feel Jesus speaking to your heart right now, don't delay. Say this prayer now!

Dear Jesus, I believe that You died for my sins and rose on the third day. I confess to You that I am a sinner. I need Your love and forgiveness. Come into my life, forgive my sins and give me eternal life. I now confess You are my Lord and Savior. Thank You for my salvation! I walk in Your peace and joy from this day forward. Amen.

I pray that you won't have to go through the extremely difficult trials that I've been through, but I pray that you will receive God's miracle-working power in your life just as I have. God bless you, and if you have said this prayer, I'll see you in paradise.

May There Be a Blessing Added to All Who Read This Book.

In Jesus' Name, Amen.

About The Author

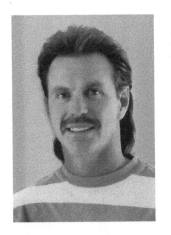

Danny Cox was called by God to be an Evangelist while serving time in prison. Since then he has been credentialed by Assemblies of God as an Evangelist and a Correctional Chaplain. He is President of DC Ministries.

With additional skills in construction, Danny has been on mission trips to China and Peru to help remodel an orphanage and a church. During this time he was able to smuggle many bibles into China and preach the Gospel through interpreters.

Although Danny preaches and gives his testimony wherever God sends him, his passion is to reach those in prison for Jesus.

Danny has been called to give his testimony of God's miracle working power in his life and to reach the lost and hurting as well as those who need a fresh word from God. His passionate testimony inspires Christians and non-Christians alike.

High On A Lie is available as an Audio Book narrated by Danny to reach blind inmates. This book will also be available in Spanish very soon.

Fold and tear along dotted line and mail

DECISION

TODAY IS THE DAY!

❑ Yes, Danny! I have made a decision to accept Jesus Christ as my personal Savior today. Please pray for me and my family.

❑ Yes, Danny! I am an inmate and I have made a decision to accept Jesus Christ as my personal Savior today. Please pray for me and my family.

_____

NAME—(please print)

PRAYER REQUEST OR COMMENTS:

_____

_____

_____

_____

_____

_____

Continue on back if needed

Mail form to:

DC Ministries
P.O. Box 353
Troy, IL 62294

Fold and tear along dotted line and mail

If you have enjoyed this book, or if it has impacted your life,
we would like to hear from you.

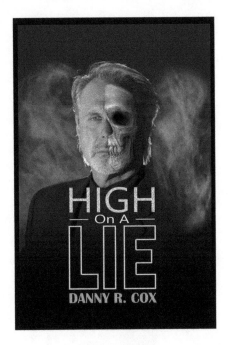

For additional copies of this book, prayers, CDs, DVDs, sermons,
or to schedule Danny for a speaking engagement -

Please contact us at:
DC Ministries
P.O. Box 353
Troy, IL 62294
Or email us at highonalie@gmail.com

CPSIA information can be obtained
at www.ICGtesting.com
Printed in the USA
FSHW020927160419